CHOICE GUIDE TO YORK, U.K.

by

Charles Patmore

2018 Edition

Published by Choice Guides
choiceguides@btinternet.com

First published as a Kindle e-book, 2011.

Published as a Paperback, May 2017

Last updated in October 2018

Obtaining this book
Both this paperback and the Kindle e-book edition can be bought on-line from Amazon. For multiple copies of this paperback or to retail, contact via e-mail address above.

If you like this book
Please post a review on either
https://www.amazon.co.uk/dp/1521325251,
https://www.amazon.com/dp/1521325251
or your own country's branch of Amazon.

ABOUT THIS GUIDE BOOK

Chapters One and Three cover respectively York Minster and the City Walls, York's two largest treasures. They go into great detail, such that you could walk round with this book in hand like a guided walk.

Chapter Two covers other historic buildings open to the public, plus quaint features of York most famous old streets, a history walk on York's green outer fringes and a visit to the nearby stately home, Beningbrough Hall. Chapter Four covers the many museums in York or nearby. For each entry in these chapters there is:

- A very brief description to show you whether you wish to read further.
- Later on, enough detailed information for you to decide whether to visit, plus points of interest to look out for during a visit.
- The phone number and website alongside the address, plus opening times and prices.
- A map reference and any nearby places of interest.
- Always there's a postcode for driving by SatNav or navigating by SmartPhone on foot.

The entry prices listed for the above are always the lowest option. Sometimes you will initially be asked for a slightly higher price, which includes 'Gift Aid'. The latter is a small donation added to the core price which, for UK taxpayers, can be amplified by government funding. If anyone does not wish to add this donation, just say that you don't want to 'Gift Aid' and you will then be charged the price listed in this book.

Chapter Five covers much miscellaneous practical information – scan the sub-headings in the Contents list.

A map of York is at the very end for quick reference.

West Front of York Minster, largest medieval cathedral in Britain and second largest in Europe

CONTENTS

Chapter Five: Additional Information **137**

Adam & Eve meet that serpent: Minster West Front

CHAPTER ONE
YORK MINSTER: A DETAILED GUIDE

What's in this chapter

Everything you need to know to enjoy a trip round York Minster, Britain's largest cathedral by far, which also has one of the most harmonious, graceful interiors. Details of:

- Famous medieval stained glass windows.
- Quirky carvings of comic people and creatures in the stonework here and there.
- Interesting tombs, some quite entertaining.
- Underneath the Minster – remains from the Roman fortress and the Minster's treasure collection.

Contact details

Address: York Minster, York YO1 7JN

Phone: 0844 939 0011

Website: **www.yorkminster.org/**

Location: Map – D2.

Nearby: **Treasurer's House**, **St William's College**

Planning your visit

- A bright day hugely enhances the stained glass and carvings inside the cathedral.
- Go before mid-afternoon, when parts of the Choir sometimes close
- Binoculars reveal beautiful details of carving and stained glass high up – and the gargoyles high up outside.
- At the very least you need an hour. If you appreciate medieval buildings, you may need well over three hours. (The new 'Orb' stained glass exhibition can absorb glass-lovers for a good hour on its own.)

- Monday – Saturday 9 am – 5 pm, all year round. Sundays: early afternoon only.
- Prices: £10 for adults, £9 for seniors and students, and free for up to 4 accompanied under 16s. This ticket now gives unlimited repeat visits for 12 months and includes underground areas like crypt and treasury.
- Climbing the central tower costs £5 extra for all ages (except those under 8, who aren't allowed to try).

Guided tours
Approximately on the hour, there are excellent free guided tours of the main Minster (excluding crypt). These last around an hour and a quarter.

Exterior
Before entering, it's worth looking at the exterior of the West Front, where the visitor entrance point is now located (photo, page 4).

Round the arch above the West Front's central door are beautiful stone carvings. On its left are carvings of Adam and Eve. Old Testament Bible stories continue all the way round the arch. On the right side, spot Noah's Ark and Samson pulling down the temple.

Stepping back, see the flowing, heart-shaped tracery of the famous West Window, sometimes called 'The Heart of Yorkshire'. It was completed in 1338.

High up, there are gargoyles and weird creatures carved all over the West Front and its two towers. And they are gesturing, yawning or even vomiting on you. On the right hand buttress of the tower on your right, the first gargoyle

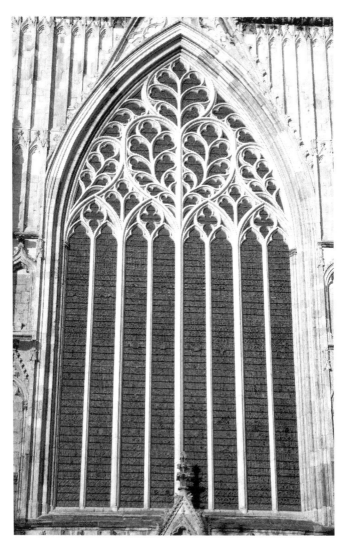

'Heart of Yorkshire' window, 1338 AD,
Minster West Front

Wild Things high on the Minster's north-west tower – binoculars will help you see them. Other wild things sometimes on this tower are a pair of nesting peregrine falcons.

Noah launches that dove, watched by a giraffe:
central portal, Minster West Front

up is a fellow with three fingers down his throat, trying to throw up on you. The most extraordinary figures are a line of faces running across the whole West Front, just below the castellated stone frieze above the West Window. Binoculars show these more clearly.

On your left is the beautiful Dean's Park.

When you approach the Minster's South Transept main entrance, on your right is a statue of Roman Emperor Constantine, who was based in York, and, almost behind you, a pillar from the old Roman fortress. The Minster is built on the heart of the Roman fortress and you can visit Roman remains in the Minster's underground areas.

Constantine camps outside the Minster,
a reminder of the Roman fort it replaced

History

Today's Minster was built gradually between 1100 and 1472. The underground Norman Crypt is the earliest part. The Transepts are largely 13th century. The Nave and Choir are mainly 14th century, while the central tower and the Great East Window are 15th century. For more on the

Minster's history, there's an excellent chart next to the north-west pillar under the central tower. (If you stand under the central tower and look towards the stone screen with the statues of kings, you are facing due east. So the pillar with this chart is on your left and slightly behind you.)

The Nave

The Nave is the half of the cathedral on the west side of the central tower. Some things you may notice in the Nave:

The Dragon's Head, half way up the north wall, was probably a crane for lifting a high, heavy font cover from the font which once stood below. In the central niche of the gallery right opposite, there's the dragon's opposite number - St George.

On each side of the West Door are six headless modern sculptures in niches. Each is holding a pair of gold semaphore bats which look like haloes. Their semaphore message reads: 'Christ is here'.

Walking along the Nave's North Aisle, the sixth window from the West Front is the 'Bell Founder's Window' – a gift from a medieval bell manufacturer. It has many images of bells. The furthest pictorial panel on the right shows molten red metal pouring from a furnace for casting a bell.

On the window to the west of this, there are monkeys in gold and brown all around the borders of many of the panels. See the little strip of stained glass at the bottom of the furthest left window panel. Some monkeys are carrying a dead comrade on a funeral bier.

North Transept

Military chapel of St John
At the end of the Nave's north aisle, on the edge of the North Transept, is the military chapel of St John. It was here that in August 2006 the Archbishop of York lived for a week in a tent, fasting and praying, during his Prayer Vigil in protest at Israeli air raids on Lebanon. Just inside the chapel, on your right and on the floor behind an iron grille, is a grim 1425 stone effigy of the decaying corpse of a Cathedral Treasurer.

The Five Sisters window
If you look northwards in the North Transept, you face five dramatically tall, elegant, slim 'lancet' windows. These are the famous 'Five Sisters', completed in 1260, one of the earliest very large stained glass creations in the world. They are made with 'grisaille' glass, a sombre mosaic of translucent pieces of thick, greeny grey glass, which preceded proper stained glass. There are more than 100,000 of these glass fragments here.

Automaton Clock
Next to a clock on the near side of the east wall of the North Transept, is a historic automaton from 1528 - every 15 minutes two knights in armour strike the chimes with their hammers. They are known as Gog and Magog.

St Nicholas Chapel
In the chapel next to Gog and Magog, on the modern kneelers are cheerful depictions of the Twelve Days of Christmas. Match up the kneelers to the lines of the song.

Astronomical Clock
Near the passage to the Chapter House is the complex modern Astronomical Clock, an RAF memorial to World

War Two. Here you can read hard-to-understand information about an even harder-to-understand object.

Chapter House

Along the passage from the North Transept, spot the various 'Green Man' carvings. The Chapter House's 13th century doors are splendid. High on the right-hand door a metal bird is flying out from the swirling metalwork design.

The Chapter House was for cathedral business meetings and, as such, is not consecrated. The medieval English parliament repeatedly met here under Edward II and Edward III, who used York as a northern capital, while leading long wars against Scotland. Around 1310 it hosted a long-running church tribunal investigating heresy charges against the Knights Templar, victims of an international persecution campaign.

The 13th century vault is wooden and suspended from the roof, hence no central column. A model shows how the roof is constructed out of huge oak timbers.

Sit back in one of the canons' seats and absorb the calm beauty of the geometric patterns which pervade the glowing stained glass windows and radiate from the wonderful Victorian tiling across the eight-sided floor.

The carved figures on the canopies
York's eight-sided Chapter House is famous for the myriad tiny faces and creatures carved on the stone canopies over the canons' seats around the walls. There are 237 little faces altogether. Going round clockwise from the left…

- The first side has some particularly expressive faces. Between the third and fourth stalls from your left, on a capital of a rear pillar there's a happy-looking couple.

- On the second side from the left, near the middle is a horrific image of a hawk blinding a woman.
- On the fourth side, directly opposite the Chapter House's entrance, several figures are grimacing and pulling their mouths open, as if with toothache. These are in the canopies above the seats for senior clergymen and this might be deliberate mockery. Also, above the fourth stall from the left are some very striking faces - including a strange, triple-faced woman.
- On this fourth side, there are some particularly beautiful leaf patterns on the stone capitals above the slim dark marble pillars. And beautiful carved stone pendants above the third stall from your left.

The mystery acoustics of the Chapter House
If two people sit in stalls directly opposite each other, one can be heard by the other right across the Chapter House, even when speaking quietly.

Under the central tower

Returning to the centre of the Minster, there's a wonderful view up to the light white ceiling of the Central Tower, richly decorated with gilded bosses. Above you stands 16000 tonnes of Tower masonry, borne on those massive pillars.

The Kings on the Choir Screen:
The stone choir screen mostly dates from 1440-60. All but one of the 15 statues of kings are original and show how medieval craftsmen depicted their own kings. See the detail on their robes and crowns. Richard I has a sweet little purse on a buckle with an animal face - the sort of thing which nowadays a kindly mum might craft for a child.

From William I to Edward III, medieval sculptors have dished out variations on one of three standard royal looks -

The Minster's north side.
The pointed building is the Chapter House.

Delicate carved stonework round a Minster archway

though Stephen gets a distinctive natty short skirt, sometimes said to reflect aspersions on his right to the throne. But the most recent kings - Richard II, Henry IV and Henry V - each get a face which is genuinely individual.

The only statue, which isn't medieval, is Henry VI on your furthest right. His original statue was removed after the Protestant Reformation because some people regarded this scholarly, unassertive, twice deposed king as some sort of saint. It was only statues of saints which the early Protestants targeted, since they opposed saint-worship. But there was no risk that the other kings could ever be mistaken for saints.

Third from the right is Henry IV – spot the shifty-looking cat stalking a mouse in the little gilded frieze of carved foliage under his feet. Under some other kings too, little carved creatures are lurking in the same spot.
Along the top of the screen is a row of exquisite angels with musical instruments – a cello, a triangle, cymbals for instance. The ninth angel from your left is playing bagpipes.

North Choir aisle and Choir

Tombs, Toilets and Truncheons
On your left, as you enter, is the memorial to googly eyed Sir George Savile. It is the first of several 17th and 18th century memorials which bear luxuriant epitaphs, packed with superlatives, poetically affirming the admirable qualities of the deceased. Every one of them seems a paragon, totally unsurpassable in every conceivable merit. What a wonderful age to live in, when such beings strode our land! Or a wonderful age, at least, to get your epitaph written. Further along the North Choir Aisle are toilets for visitors. On the right side of their entrance, there's a surprising pair of old truncheons, one marked YMP. They are from York Minster's own tiny police force.

Archbishop Savage's chantry chapel
Soon after, on the right, is the large, beautiful, Gothic tomb of Archbishop Savage with exquisite stone carving. See the angels around the arches, who are swinging censers, and the delicate grapes and leaves in the niches. Above this tomb is a tiny canopied upstairs 'chantry' chapel - the sort where prayers for the Archbishop's soul would have been repeatedly said by a priest solely employed for this purpose.

A tomb with a tale
Next come some Elizabethan and Jacobean tombs with nicely coloured tableaux of family groups. Immediately on your left is the first of these, the Bellasis tomb, showing Bellasis, his wife in hooped skirt and three children. Not many of us get to enjoy the sight of our own tomb, but Bellasis completed this for himself nine years before he died, not trusting his son to build a grand enough monument. Above the central pilaster, a cherub is busy with a bubble blowing kit, known in those days it seems.

The St William Window's strange story
Immediately above the Bellasis tomb is the renowned, very tall, stained glass St William Window. It was created in 1414, probably by the same Coventry master craftsman who made the Great East Window. To see it properly, you need to step back into the Choir and stand near the High Altar.

The window illustrates the curious tale how William Fitzherbert became Archbishop of York twice - and ended up as St William of York.

A relative of King Stephen, the pleasure-loving William became Treasurer of York Minster by the age of 22. He sounds like one of those people to whom advancement somehow comes naturally. But when in 1143, with royal help, he became Archbishop of York, he was denounced by a puritanical Cistercian abbot as "rotten from the soles of his feet to the crown of his head". The third row from the bottom of the window shows clergymen brandishing documents bearing the accusations of corruption which eventually got the Pope to depose William. In the right two panels is the Pope in triple tiara.

But ten years later, under a new Pope, somehow William got himself back to York as Archbishop again. You see him returning in triumph across the Ouse bridge if you look at the central strand of glass panels, fourth panel down from where the window's canopy juts out. Alas, the bridge then collapsed under the weight of onlookers. But York opinion looked firmly on the bright side. Rather than see this as divine wrath at William's re-instatement, people hailed the bridge's collapse as a saintly miracle, since no-one had actually been killed.

Not so long afterwards, however, William dropped dead after saying Mass. His supporters charged that poison had been slipped into his Mass chalice by another clergyman. Church politics rarely get more hardball.

Somehow, it was only after his death that William's saintly side really manifested. Miracles seemed just to happen around his tomb. And so he was declared a saint in 1227, as pilgrims flooded to York. Many panels in the upper window show sick or injured people touching his tomb for cures. In the lowest far left panel of the upper window, a grizzly winged demon is possessing a man – even problems like this could get sorted at this wonderful tomb! A substance began to flow from the tomb and this was hailed as fragrant, healing oil. Some window panels show people anointing themselves with this fluid or taking it home in pots. And as this oil, or whatever it was, flowed out, so pilgrims' money flowed into York.

'Shadows show the presence of light': that's the drift of the Latin on the Minster's sundial

Detail on a Minster pilaster

But the Reformation took a sour view of all this. The elaborate tomb, shown repeatedly in the upper window, was destroyed as the focus of a superstitious cult. The Minster's crypt now contains a reassembled tomb for St William, a rather more modest one.

The Choir and High Altar

In the capitals above the pillars here are some striking carvings. The choir stalls and multi-spired thrones are 19th century woodwork. They replace medieval woodwork burnt by a mad arsonist who was actually the brother of John Martin, the popular Romantic-age artist whose vast paintings of apocalyptic destruction are prominent at Tate Britain.

The Great East Window and its restoration

Behind the High Altar is the largest Gothic window in the world, larger than a tennis court. The Great East Window was made 1405-1408 by a renowned Coventry master glazier. It comprises 117 stained glass panels in rows of nine. These panels illustrate Bible stories like the Seven Days of Creation and the prophecies in the Book of Revelations.

In 2011 all the stained glass was removed from the window for a lengthy restoration process. In early 2018, the last of the cleaned and restored stained glass panels were reassembled in the window, like a giant jigsaw. The images in the panels are so much brighter and more colourful now they have been cleaned!

The touch-screen guides to the Great East Window

Facing the window, some ingenious touch-screen digital guides show close-up any stained glass panel which you select and explain its subject matter. Many panels illustrate the Book of Revelations' dread visions of the end of the world. The Four Horsemen of the Apocalypse stalk the earth and the Great Beast With Seven Heads holds sway. Remorseless angels tip vials of plagues from the sky and a whole load of Seals are broken to release a sort of medieval version of a nuclear holocaust. For each stained glass panel, the touch-screen guide offers a link to the Bible text which it illustrates.

On the touch-screen guides, you can zoom to see close-up the delicate details of the stained glass paintings which for centuries no-one has got close enough to see – beautiful, expressive faces, each wisp of saint's beard, each feather of angel's wing, each fish's scale. You can see the slim plague vial in one of those plague angels' hands and the deadly red liquid pouring out and dead fish floating in the waters below. You see exactly what the Great Beast gets up to with its seven heads: it can nibble more than one Christian priest at a time!

These touch-screen displays also include an inventive menu about arcane numerical symbolism in the window's multi-panel lay-out – numerology enthusiasts will be in, sorry, seventh heaven.

Exhibitions about the East Window restoration
While the stained glass was away for repairs, the east end of York Minster was occupied by an exhibition about the restoration process. It seems likely that some of this will remain after the window is completely installed, though it may be reduced in scale and change periodically. Some items to expect:

- Videos and displays which show how stained glass is made and how the medieval panels were restored.
- A child-friendly touch-screen which lets you colour in a window design of your choice.

- A jigsaw game about reassembling fragments of stained glass.
- A Spot the Difference game about window panels before and after restoration.

The Great East Window

South Choir Aisle

There are several tombs worth attention in the chapels on both sides of the Great East Window and also in the south choir aisle, as you walk westwards back towards the cathedral entrance.

The secret sign of the pea pod

Turning down the south choir aisle, on your right you soon reach an ancient chest for bishops' vestments. Behind this is a large marble tomb sculpture, showing a bishop in a rather theatrical pose. It's by Grinling Gibbons, best known for his fabulous woodcarving for St Pauls, London. Gibbons is said to have used a secret code to show when his work had been fairly recompensed – and when he'd encountered sharp practice. If fairly treated, he would carve an open pea pod, like that visible in the bottom right hand corner of this slab. If feeling cheated, there'd be a closed pea pod instead. So a work by Grinling Gibbons could tell posterity more about his customer than they had bargained for.

The message from the dead

On the other side of this aisle, a few tombs further on, is a tomb with a man in Elizabethan clothes, flanked by two women, and with six children below. This is Sir William Gee, who died in 1611. An intriguing inscription starts off:

> "Stay Gentle Passenger and reade
> A sentence sent thee from ye dead."

Since it's not every day that we get one of these, it's worth reading the tomb's message till the punch line at the end.

The St Cuthbert Window

Immediately above Sir William Gee's tomb is the exquisite 15th century St Cuthbert Window, which tells the life story of the seventh century saint of the Holy Island of Lindisfarne. It is so tall that you need to step into the Choir to see it properly. Though hard to spot, several panels recount St Cuthbert's dealings with birds, of whom he was a firm friend. On the Farne Islands, he created one of the world's first legal bird sanctuaries. Look at the row of glass panels immediately below the first horizontal stone bar from the top of the window. The second panel from the left shows St Cuthbert in discussion with a bird. The second from the right shows him sailing to his Farne Island hermitage.

The "excellent wife"

Continuing westwards, in the next bay but one to Sir William Gee's tomb, there's a sad tale told by the tomb of Jane Hodson, who died in 1636. Look for a classical pediment with a fiery pot above it; the inscription is in Latin but an English translation is placed below. It's another memorial which can prompt thoughts which its creator, her mournful husband, never anticipated. Her virtues were manifold, he proclaims: pious, modest, generous, good at budgeting, "a faithful wife", a "daily support" to her husband. Not least, "a fruitful mother" for she "increased the lineage of her husband by bearing 24 children", then died aged 38 (do the maths). And all this, he spells out, without ever losing her looks.

Echoes of empire

Further westwards along the South Choir Aisle (i.e further back towards the Minster's entrance) are memorials evoking life and death in Britain's imperial age - death in battle, from heatstroke or fever in hot, dusty, colonial wars in places like Sudan, South Africa, India or New Zealand. In 1870, even a Greek holiday could end in display of imperial pluck, as the memorial to young Frederick Vyner shows. Kidnapped by Greek brigands, his plaque proclaims his prayer to "die bravely as Englishmen should do."

*The Minster's south side, the 'reconciliation rose window'
in the transept's gable*

South Transept

The reconciliation rose window
The designs in the rose window were intended to represent reconciliation at the end of the bloody 15th century Wars of the Roses. Two rival branches of the royal family had been fighting for the throne: the Dukes of Lancaster (emblem Red Rose) and the Dukes of York (emblem White Rose). King Henry VII (Red Rose) had overthrown a White Rose king in the final battle of the Wars of the Roses in 1485. He then artfully married into the rival dynasty so that his heir represented both Red and White Rose claims to the throne. In the rose window, the 24 petals of the rose-shaped tracery contain alternating pairs of red roses and white roses. The rose at the centre combines white petals at the centre with red on the outside.

The children's roof boss designs

This roof was reconstructed after a fire in 1984. Some new roof bosses used designs about modern events, produced by children in a TV Blue Peter competition. Look for these four, which differ colour wise from the gold hue of the rest.

- Fairly near the north-west corner of the South Transept is a roof boss with a silver crescent moon and an astronaut (i.e. next to the nave, on the side furthest from High Altar).
- Diagonally opposite (south-east corner), is another silver hued boss with an astronaut and the earth as seen from space.
- Near the south-west corner is a boss showing the raising of the Tudor warship, the Mary Rose.
- Diagonally opposite this is the Save the Whale campaign – a whale, a diver and silver bubbles.

Climbing the Central Tower

There are usually two trips per hour up the 275 steps. You get a badge afterwards as a prize, children also.

Underground parts of the Minster

Under the Minster you can visit the Norman crypt and a new exhibition in the treasury plus Roman remains discovered among the foundations. The crypt is entered from the choir aisles; the rest from the south transept.

The Crypt

This is much the oldest part of today's Minster and has splendid patterned Norman columns. The western part of the crypt contains a recent recreation of a tomb for St William of York – he of the beautiful red and blue window and the poisoned Mass chalice.

At the eastern end (i.e. nearer the altar), look out for:
The 'Doom Stone' in the south-east corner. This Norman stone slab shows a hell scene where demons are stoking

flames and the tiny souls of sinners are peering out. Look at the right edge from sideways and you'll see a large devil's face, its nostrils being thoughtfully cleaned out by toads.

In the far north-east corner, the floor has been cut away to show the base of a Roman column in the commander's house in the 4th century Roman fortress, located exactly under where you are standing.

Among the foundations
Around the late 1960s, urgent excavations were undertaken to insert steel and concrete reinforcements under the central tower's foundations. This uncovered many traces of the old Roman fortress, immediately under the Minster, and other precursors of the present Minster. Since June 2013, a new exhibition shows the actual Roman column bases and wall foundations alongside information about the huge Roman fortress and subsequent Saxon and Norman buildings here. Displays show objects found here like coins, cloak pins, clay lamps, dice and tiles. Look out for:
- a wall from a Roman officers' mess room – still visible, some Roman military wall decor in original bright colours.
- a Roman drainage culvert, whereby, incredibly, water is still being drained from under the Minster to the Ouse.
- 'Ulph's Horn', a carved Viking drinking horn, the sort you'd expect in Valhalla.

Ulph's Horn is made from an elephant's tusk and probably reached York via the Viking colony in Sicily. Ulph was an 11th century Viking settler in Yorkshire, who worried that his sons would bicker terribly over their shares of their inheritance. So he left everything to York Minster instead, this horn included. Very wise.

A tale told in treasures

Another part of the new exhibition describes religious activities at the Minster and illustrates this through items from the cathedral's treasures. There are videos of Christian rituals, explanations of altar vessels and of a bishop's mitre, crozier and colourful vestments, and tales of York's more extraordinary Archbishops.

Look out for the amazing, Saxon 'Gospels of York'. The original book is present - and also digital copies where you can turn over some pages. We're fairly used to much later medieval book illustrations, where Gospel figures are naively placed in medieval clothes and Gothic buildings. But this pre-Norman book is so old that its pictures of clothes and architectural details are quite accurate for the Roman era when the events actually happened.

Participative exhibits

- Try your hand at building a Norman and a Gothic arch with wooden bricks – the last stage is the tricky one.
- Children can dress up as a bishop for a photo.
- A digital display lets you fit a bishop's fashion accessories into a coffin holding the skeleton of Walter de Grey. He was a famously bling, acquisitive, medieval Archbishop of York. He certainly wouldn't like to depart without his worldly goods!

Special Tours

At the South Transept information desk (where you enter) and on the Minster website you can hear about special interest tours like:

- tours of the nearby stained glass conservation workshop
- the 'Stoneyard' where stone carvings are restored
- the belfry and hidden parts of the Minster.

Exhibitions in former Bishops' Palace

Here there are sometimes exhibitions about the Minster. Now better known as the Minster Library, it's in the far corner of the lovely Dean's Garden behind the Minster. Your Minster ticket grants you access.

York Illuminations Festival 2010: giant images from the Minster's stained glass projected on to its exterior

CHAPTER TWO
YORK'S HISTORIC BUILDINGS

Historic buildings in York, open to the public

- *Treasurer's House:* beautiful 17th century house with famous Roman ghost location (National Trust) **p.34**
- *Bar Convent:* 18th century 'secret convent' with museum about persecution of Catholics **p.38**
- *Merchant Adventurers' Guild Hall:* grand medieval hall used by this mysterious guild **p.42**
- *Roman Bath:* small underground bath house from York's Roman era **p.45**
- *Fairfax House:* Georgian house with Georgian antique collection. **p.45**
- *York Council's Guildhall:* restored 15th century hall with entertaining roof boss designs **p. 47**
- *All Saints Church:* York's finest medieval parish church with famous 'End of the World' stained glass window **p. 49**
- *York's old streets:* Stonegate, Petergate, the Shambles - spot the trade symbols on old shops, the hidden 'snickelway' alleys and a whole load of statues of cats **p. 51**
- *Barley Hall:* grand town house of medieval social climber. **p.56**

Cafés, restaurants and pubs in historic buildings

- *St Williams College:* 15th century timbered building with indoor restaurant and courtyard café tables, just behind Minster **p.58**
- *Black Swan Inn:* 15th century timbered home, now a pub with food and folk music **p.59**
- *Spurriergate Centre:* child-friendly cafeteria in former medieval church, centre of York **p.59**

- *King's Manor:* lunch place inside former royal palace and seat of government **p.60**
- *Grand Assembly Rooms:* Italian restaurant in Georgian York's purpose-built venue for balls **p.60**
- *Other historic places for food or drink:* medieval and Victorian pubs **p.61**

Beyond York's City Walls
- *Nuclear War Observation Bunker:* secret till recently, now York's newest English Heritage attraction **p.62**
- *Holgate Windmill:* close to the above, a beautiful, five sail 1770 windmill **p.65**
- *Riverside and racecourse history walk:* Georgian riverside parade, racecourse, old gallows site and, a chocolate baron's home and garden **p.67**
- *Beningbrough Hall:* smart Georgian stately home (National Trust), 10 miles from York and easily reached by bus or bike. Child-friendly ethos with participative art displays. All-day restaurant **p.73**

HISTORIC BUILDINGS IN YORK, OPEN TO THE PUBLIC

Treasurer's House
In a nutshell
The Treasurer's House is a beautiful old building which showcases the antique collection and creative fantasies of Frank Green, a wealthy Edwardian style-obsessive. He was so flamboyant and eccentric that no novelist would dare to invent him. York's most famous ghost sighting is also commemorated here.

Contact details
Address: Minster Yard, York, North Yorkshire YO1 7JL
Phone: 01904 624247
Website:
www.nationaltrust.org.uk/treasurers-house-york

Location: Map – right side of D2, just behind the Minster's East End.

Places nearby: **Minster**, **St William's College**.

Opening times, prices and facilities

- Open daily, 1 March – 31 October inclusive. 11 am – 4.30 pm. In November and December from Thursday to Sunday only.
- Prices: Adult £8.10. Child £4.05. Family tickets £20.25. Free to National Trust members.
- Tea room.

House, Ghosts and Garden

In 1897 this 17th century mansion was bought by Frank Green, the ultra-dapper playboy grandson of a Yorkshire self-made businessman, who had left him a fortune from re-using hot air from heating boilers. Frank Green then beautified the House and stocked it lavishly with antiques.

He was more of an arty stage-set designer than a scholarly expert on historical styles. He would readily change the house to suit his ideas for a good vista or to fit in a particular antique. For instance, he acquired an old German clock with a massive pendulum, over 4 metres (13 ft) long. So he cut a hole in the floor to fit the pendulum and you see it swinging on the storey below the actual clock.

Some of Green's ideas are very beautiful, like the dramatically spacious 'medieval' entrance hall. He worked obsessively to get the look he wanted. You see studs set in the floor to show where every chair should go and servants were ordered to maintain these precise arrangements.

You'll hear much entertaining information about Frank Green's extravagance. A confirmed bachelor, he kept an entourage of 15 servants. There are photos of him posing with them, pompous and self-absorbed and terrifyingly well-dressed. Guides tell you about his six Rolls Royces, his lavish fancy dress parties and visits from royalty, and how this fussy, fastidious man would have his laundry sent to London.

He assembled a fleet of early motor caravans, one modelled as a dining room, another as a bathroom, plus a bedroom, a sitting room and so on. When this mansion-on-wheels convoy set off for the Continent, it returned rather swiftly. No ferry could be found which was large enough.

The famous Roman ghosts at the Treasurer's House
Ghostly Roman soldiers have been sighted repeatedly at the Treasurer's House, which is inside York's Roman military base. Once a Roman soldier intruded on one of Frank Green's fancy-dress parties but was initially mistaken for a rather difficult guest. The most famous sighting occurred in 1953 when a heating engineer in the cellar saw 20 dejected-looking Roman soldiers led by a bugler. You can visit this cellar on a special tour and hear the tale. Alternatively, a video in the display room about the House's history shows both the cellar and the heating engineer himself telling his story.

The Garden
At the front of the Treasurer's House, facing the Minster, is a small but exquisite garden with statues and fountain in the 17th century style. It is usually open to the public free of charge. For a moment of peaceful rest, it is one of the loveliest places in York.

Treasurer's House

Fountain in Treasurer's House
garden

The Bar Convent

In a nutshell

This building tells the extraordinary story of a secret convent for Catholic nuns, dating from when Catholicism was illegal, which hid behind the front of being a girls' boarding school. The convent began in the late 17th century. As it grew, the building's 18th century roof was carefully constructed to conceal the new chapel dome, lest people suspect that it was more than a girls' school. Today it remains a convent, though since 1985 separate from its flourishing girls' school. Its unusual museum commemorates Catholic resistance to persecution in England.

Contact details

Address: The Bar Convent, 17 Blossom Street, York, YO24 1AQ

Phone: 01904 643 238

Website: **www.bar-convent.org.uk**

Location: Map – B6.

Places nearby: **Micklegate Bar Museum** . Rail Station.

Opening times, prices and facilities

- Museum usually open Mondays to Saturdays 10 am - 5 pm for most of the year. Usually closed on Bank Holidays, throughout Easter, and during the Christmas / New Year period.
- Admission costs £5 for adults, £4 for pensioners and students, £2 for children aged 6 – 15.
- Group guided tours can be booked in advance.
- There is a café. Also 18 rooms for Bed & Breakfast - the Convent is near the rail station. For descriptions and booking, see Convent's website.

The Museum

The Ground Floor section tells the tale of the secret life of England's persecuted Catholics during the 16th century, when Catholic priests and anyone helping them were liable to treason charges. Through keyhole shaped panels, as soon as you enter, you can spy old prints of grim scenes of the times. Wall charts tell the stories of some of the 36 Catholics who were executed for their faith in Yorkshire during the 16th and 17th centuries. Mostly they were hanged near York's Knavesmire racecourse and their bodies disemboweled and chopped into quarters. A reliquary in the museum shows priests' bones retrieved in secret from two such butcherings.

The museum gives a fascinating picture of the work of undercover Catholic priests during this period, who risked death on the Knavesmire in order to minister to secret Catholic loyalists. Look out for a miniature altar, disguised as a mantelpiece ornament, and a tiny horn Mass chalice which could be hidden inside it. There's also a bed headboard with a hidden hinged shelf which can be swiftly lowered to form an instant altar and altarpiece for an illegal Mass. Look out for the set of miniaturised church vestments which an undercover priest could carry hidden on him, so he'd always have the right colour for church festivals.

Also on the ground floor is a delightful very short audio-visual display which tells the Bar Convent's story in a nutshell. Find the magic lantern and turn its handle to start this display.

Upstairs the museum presents the history of the convent. It grew from a rather feminist Catholic religious order created by Mary Ward in the early 17th century - in defiance of the Pope. She insisted that her nuns gave direct help to the public and not seclude themselves completely. So she got

The Bar Convent's hidden chapel - from the era when Catholics were persecuted in England

From the Bar Convent's museum, a secret altar for an illegal Catholic Mass. Flip up the hinged shelf and it's just an ordinary piece of furniture!

persecuted by both Pope and Protestants. On display is a set of fifty 17th century paintings of incidents in the life of Mary Ward. Below is a touch-screen display which offers close-ups and detailed explanation of each painting.

Upstairs too is information about more recent history of the Bar Convent and video interviews with today's nuns, describing their present life here and what it means to them. Quite remarkable – the oldest living convent in England and still very much alive.

The Chapel

The Chapel was built in 1769. Since Catholic services were illegal till 1791, it was carefully constructed within the 'school' so that its dome would not be visible from the street. There were eight exits to enable speedy departure of priests, should the authorities arrive. In the far-left corner of the Chapel you can see a secret exit tunnel under the floor. The Chapel is dazzling white and gold, bright and beautiful in a very graceful Classical way.

The Hand

Sometimes it is hidden in a little cupboard in the Chapel and sometimes it is on full display in a glass reliquary on the altar. The severed hand of Saint Margaret Clitherow is a most unsettling sight, vividly recalling the savage 1586 martyrdom of this pious York housewife for practicing Catholicism according to her conscience. There is still flesh on her hand and her fingers claw forward, as if beckoning you. She was publicly crushed to death in the most horrible way possible, after a trial in York's Guildhall. An information panel in the downstairs part of the museum tells her story thoroughly, complete with a grim old print of her execution. Other places in York, where her martyrdom is remembered: her public shrine inside 35 The Shambles, and a plaque on Ouse Bridge, where her crushing under weights took place (near Micklegate riverbank, on the pavement on the downstream side).

Merchant Adventurers Hall

In a nutshell
This splendid, perfectly preserved medieval building takes you into the world of York's medieval guilds, which today still organise York's Mystery Plays. Built in 1360, it has, ever since, been the headquarters of York's leading guild, a mysterious network of insiders which has held great power in York. History comes alive in this beautiful place, as you learn how the Merchant Adventurers gave charitably with one hand but bullied with the other.

Contact details
Address: The Merchant Adventurers' Hall, Fossgate, York YO1 9XD
Phone: 01904 654818
Website: **www.theyorkcompany.co.uk/**

Location: Map – E4. *Places nearby*: **Jorvik**, **Fairfax House**

Opening times, prices and facilities
- March – October, open daily, Mondays – Thursdays 9 am – 5 pm, Friday & Saturday 9 – 3.30 pm, Sunday 11 am – 4 pm.
- November – February, open Monday – Thursday, 10 am – 4 pm. Friday & Saturday, 10 am - 3.30 pm.
- Closed between Christmas and New Year.
- Prices: Adult £6.50. Concessions £5.50. Accompanied under 16s, free.

The Merchant Adventurers and their Hall
One face of the Merchant Adventurers was as medieval merchants who traded Yorkshire wool for imports from Europe. They supplied each other with loans for such

ventures and insurance against shipwrecks. Some were imaginative entrepreneurs – a 16th century Adventurer founded Croft's Port in Oporto, for instance. The magnificent, wooden beamed, banqueting hall on the upper floor is where they held grand dinners and you see their portraits on the walls and their fur-lined robes. You also see a painting of today's Merchant Adventurers, for they continue as an influential network of the Great and the Good in York – membership most definitely by invitation only.

Another face of this guild made them hated by many York shopkeepers. From medieval times, the Crown gave them government-like powers as inspectors of all other York tradesmen. On display are the weights and measures against which they checked those of other businesses. Incredibly, till 1830 no-one else was allowed to sell foreign imports in York, apart from fish and salt. The Merchant Adventurers held trials in this Hall and imposed fines on shopkeepers who sold things like tea without paying them for a licence. On the upper floor, you can see their judge's throne. The Hall's interesting audio-guide recounts how one 18th century shopkeeper resisted such demands for money.

Yet another face of the organisation was charitable work. Downstairs was a care home for 13 poor people with infirmities. There was a free apothecary service which gave medicines to hundreds of poor people. If you gave the Guild a donation, in return you received 'free treatment' tickets which you could give to poor people of your choice. Downstairs is a 19th century board which lists charities like interest-free business start-up loans and schooling for poor children.

Some other things worth looking out for:

- Upstairs, in the Committee Room, there's an apprentice's contract whose tough terms show how guilds controlled even whether their members could marry. Guilds made life easier for their established members through controlling competition on price, quality or marketing, like a modern professional association. Exacting rules made it easy to discourage any newcomer from rocking the boat.

- Downstairs are banners from 20 York guilds. Before reading the labels, try to decipher the trade symbols on each banner.

- Downstairs, in the chapel at the back, is a most unusual sundial. It is actually embedded into the very top central panel of the stained glass window.

- For children, there's a game on a digital monitor downstairs whereby you test your acumen as a medieval merchant adventurer. You choose goods to buy in York to sell in various continental ports, then refill your cargo ship for return to York. An optional button offers a whisper from Guild members as to what sells well in particular places. See then how Guild membership can boost your medieval profits!

Aside from the latter, there's not that much here likely to interest children.

Roman Bath

In a nutshell

Under this modern pub is a Roman bath house not discovered till 1929. You pay at the bar, then head down steps on the far right. In a large cavern-like space under the pub, you see the underfloor pillars under one of the hot rooms, where very hot air from the furnace circulated. This visit is interesting, short and low cost and in a central place which you'll walk past anyway. Not to be missed! For more information:

www.roman-britain.org/places/york_baths.htm

Contact details

Address: The Roman Bath Public House, 9 St Sampson's Square, YO1 8RN
Phone: (01904) 620455
Website:
www.sandm.freeserve.co.uk/romanbath/main.html

Location: Map – bottom right of D3.
Places nearby: **Stonegate**, **Barley Hall**.

Opening times and prices
- Access is usually 10 am – 7 pm.
- Prices: Adult £3.50. Concessions £2.50. Children £2. Families £9.

Fairfax House

In a nutshell

Fairfax House will delight lovers of antiques or Georgian style. It's an elegant Georgian town house which was sumptuously prepared as a dowry – but for a marriage which got traumatically called off. Abandoned as a result, it decayed. But it was restored in the 1980s with scholarly attention to Georgian style and now also showcases the antique collection of York chocolate magnate, Noel Terry.

Contact details
Address: Fairfax House, Castlegate, York YO1 9RN
Phone: (01904) 655543
Website: **www.fairfaxhouse.co.uk/**

Location: Map – E5.
Places nearby: **Cliffords Tower**, **Castle Museum** & **Jorvik**.

Opening times, prices and facilities
- Open nearly all year – from 6 February till 31 December, except for Christmas.
- Open Tuesday – Saturday 10 am – 5 pm. Sunday 11 am – 4 pm. Mondays open only for 1 hour guided tours at 11 am and 2 pm (arrive 10 minutes early).
- Prices: Adult £7.50. Concessions £6. Child £3. Each ticket can be reused all year.

What it's like
Key features are beautifully ornamented plaster ceilings and marble fireplaces, marquetry furniture, clocks, and escritoires in Chinoiserie style or with concealed drawers. One theme is recreations of Georgian food presentation. There's a dinner table laid out Georgian style.

Two curiosities:
- The kitchen has a clever system whereby hot air rotated a fan in the chimney to drive a power train which rotated both a spit and a pot over the fire.
- There's a specially high four-poster bed which enables one to look down on one's servants even when in bed. But this requires steps to get into bed. Artfully concealed inside these steps, hey presto, is a commode.

York Council's Guildhall

In a nutshell
This is a much-restored medieval hall with colourful, entertaining roof bosses, which is attached to York Council's former HQ in the centre of York. The future of the complex is currently being debated. For the time being, quite often you'll get access, if the hall is not in use. There's no entry charge.

Address: The Guildhall, St Helen's Square, York YO1 9QN
Phone: (01904) 613161
Website:
www.york.gov.uk/council/offices/buildings/the_guildhall/

Location: Map – C4.
Places nearby: **Museum Gardens**, **Stonegate**, **Visit York**.

Opening times, price and access
 You can visit on spec. As mentioned above, access is somewhat unpredictable. Sometimes there are tours on Saturdays.

Walk down the long, arched tunnel, near where Coney Street, St Helen's Square and Lendal join. Then follow the signed passage on your right into the Council Offices.

If the Guildhall is not in use, you sometimes get a 4-page leaflet to guide you round it.

Free entry.

What it's like
This 15th century Gothic hall has long been the scene of important York Council ceremonies, banquets and major trials. It was here in the 16th century that the horrible trial

took place of the Catholic martyr, St. Margaret Clitherow, whose shrine can be visited in the Shambles and whose severed hand is now sometimes displayed at the **Bar Convent**.

The hall was severely damaged by a fire bomb during World War II and today's massive timber pillars and the many amusing, carved and painted faces on the roof bosses are reconstructions. The stained glass Gothic window is likewise new and the Guildhall leaflet explains themes from York's history in its panels.

You may also be able to enter Committee Room One – in the far-left corner as you face the stained glass window. It is a beautiful 15th century paneled room which was undamaged by the bombing. Here there are more strange faces on wooden bosses – a Green Man and a chap with two tongues, for instance. Behind some paneling are two secret passages, which are sometimes demonstrated during organised tours. During the Civil War, this room was where Parliament's agents spent a week counting out the gigantic 'incentive payment' required by their Scottish 'allies'. In return Parliament received hopelessly inept assistance and the Scots later changed sides anyway.

In Committee Room One, the Guildhall

There are too many to detail. *Visit York* provides a leaflet about 13 medieval churches within the City Walls. The most interesting are often located where you'll notice them anyway - like St Michael le Belfry next the Minster or Holy Trinity, visible from Goodramgate. But the very best church needs mentioning since it is hidden away in little North Street.

All Saints Church, North Street
Address: All Saints Church, North Street, York YO1 6JD
Phone: (01904) 706047
Website: **allsaints-northstreet.org.uk**

Location: Map - C4.
It's not marked on the map but it's at the corner between Tanner Row and North Street, directly opposite the City Screen Cinema shown on the map across the river. Do not confuse with another All Saints on the Minster side of the river!
North Street runs along the river between Ouse Bridge (leads to Micklegate) and Lendal Bridge (leads to the Rail Station).

Opening times
- Open Monday to Saturday, 10am - 6pm in Summer, 10am - 3pm in Winter

What's in this church
Most famous item is the forbidding 15th century 'Pricke of Conscience' window, which shows 15 events leading up to the end of the world. It seems that a tsunami, then earthquakes are coming, then a great firestorm, leaving dazed humans hiding in holes. Text boards supply the ancient Doom Poem which it illustrates, a window panel

per verse. It's at the far end of the north aisle (left side of altar).

On its left, the 14th century 'Corporal Acts of Mercy' window includes fascinating details like medieval disability aids and a medieval bedspread.

A fabulous 15th century wooden roof with beautifully carved and coloured angels. Some hold musical instruments. One angel gently lifts a human soul aloft in a sort of napkin.

The wooden screens, whilst modern craftsmanship, are some of the best Gothic wood designs in England.

The cell of a 15th century hermit prophetess, expanded in Edwardian times for early 20th century hermits at this very Anglo-Catholic church. Viewable on occasion only.

For enthusiasts for old churches, that's just the start of All Saints' treasures.

Turmoil in the seas as the world ends.
From the 'Pricke of Conscience' window, All Saints Church

YORK'S OLD STREETS

In a nutshell
York has some charming streets of very old houses – and shops which still carry the symbols which signalled their trade to people who could not read. Here's how to recognise interesting features of these old streets.

Where to look
York's best medieval streets are Stonegate, Petergate, the Shambles and parts of Goodramgate - all close together. Stonegate and Petergate are in the Map square D3, Goodramgate in E3, and the Shambles in E3 & 4.

Across the river is Micklegate (Map squares B & C 5) with some of the best 18th and 19th century houses. Bootham (Map square C2) has fine 18th and 19th century houses.

Dating the old houses
The old houses here were built in different centuries and many shopfronts are 19th century additions. But there's a rough rule of thumb whereby you can date many houses.

At the end of Stonegate closest to the Minster, from No. 60 – No. 48, you can see a block of typical 14th / 15th century houses (though with 19th century shop fronts).
- They have floors which jut out over the street.
- Plaster covers the walls.
- Sometimes you can see a frame of massive timbers under the plaster.

Houses like this usually range from 14th – 16th century.

Just round the corner in High Petergate, at Numbers 23 – 27, there's a completely different look.
- Flat walls in red brick – no floors sticking out.
- Elegantly proportioned large rectangular windows
- Much is symmetrical.

Houses like this are usually 18th century. This row was built 1700 -1779.

Old street features
In these High Petergate houses, just mentioned, on the left of the door of No. 23, there's an iron socket for extinguishing the fiery torch which people carried along unlit streets at night.

Next door but one, at No. 27 High Petergate, just above the door is a Sun Insurance Company 'Fire Mark'. Before public fire brigades, this mark meant this insurance company's private fire brigade should fight any fire there.

In the 15th century, The Shambles was a street entirely of butchers. From No. 7 – No. 13, the shops still have butchers' counters and some meat hooks. No.12 is a lovely old sweet shop.

Several shops show old trade signs. In Stonegate, booksellers and printers were prominent.
- At the Minster end of Stonegate, up on the wall of Minster Gates is Minerva, goddess of wisdom and learning, with her owl.
- There's a bible hanging over No. 35 Stonegate because it was once a bookshop.
- No. 33 Stonegate has a little red devil, the sign for a printer.
- No. 76 Low Petergate has a man in a curious feathered headdress – local thoughts on what a Native American might look like. It's an early tobacconist's sign, since tobacco came from America.

Minerva and the Native American are shown on the next page.

Minerva, goddess of wisdom, promotes nearby bookshops

Shop sign for an early tobacconist, 76 Low Petergate

York's 'cat sculpture trail'

More recent street decorations include various cat sculptures on buildings. There's a trail leaflet with a map about 17 cats to find around central York. You can download it from:

www.yorkluckycats.co.uk/york-cat-trail.html

Or collect it from the York Glass shop, 34 The Shambles, who sell glass 'York Lucky Cats' in each month's birthstone colour.

The best known cat sculpture is the cat stalking the bird along a roof ridge in Kings Square. Another prominent cat is clinging to a high building front, near where Low Ousegate, downstream side, reaches Ouse Bridge. Nearby is a pal, chained to a high window sill. Look at the third and fourth properties from the bridge (bottom of map square D4.).

'Snickelways'

Next to No. 83 Low Petergate is an alley signed 'Lunds Court formerly Mad Alice Lane'. This is a 'snickelway', one of a hidden network of short-cuts round old Yorkshire towns. Some people find these alleys quaint; others think them dingy. See where this one takes you. You'll find more if you keep trying openings to alleys in York's Old Town. There's a popular book about York's snickelways.

Old houses which you can enter

No. 35, The Shambles is now a public shrine to St Margaret Clitherow, who lived in this street though in a different house. She was martyred horribly in 1586 for loyalty to the Catholic religion. Her story is summarised in panels on the walls. Fuller, grimmer detail is on display at the Bar Convent – see the entry in this book.

Dating old York houses: left hand shop shows the 14th – 16th century look, while right hand building is typical 18th century. Page 51 lists common clues about dates.

No. 19 Stonegate has fabulous carvings on its wooded beams and delightful little latticed windows. It is mainly 15th century and perhaps the finest building in Stonegate. In 2016 it became a spectacular shop selling high quality, traditional German Christmas decorations – well worth a visit to see these too (details in 'Christmas Season' in Ch 5.)

Barley Hall, off Stonegate, YO1 8AR. Between 31 and 33 Stonegate is a lane marked 'Coffee Yard'. Walk down it and on your left a modern plate glass window displays Barley Hall's medieval dining hall. For an entrance fee you can tour the whole wood-beamed, rambling medieval house. Built in 1360, it became the swanky home of a 15th century relentless social climber. Nowadays some rooms usually host exhibitions on life in medieval York, while others are furnished medieval-style. There are children's activities, like period games of skittles and hoop-la and sometimes dressing up in medieval clothes. Also, there are changing exhibitions. Repeatedly these have featured actual costumes from well-known historical films or TV series. Till March 2018 you can see lead characters' costumes from the BBC TV 'Wolf Hall' series, set in the reign of Henry VIII. The Brown Look seems to have been the thing for Henry's entourage. Whether it's Henry himself, his queens or his ministers, everyone's wearing brown from top to toe!

Opening times: open every day, 10 am – 5pm during April to October inclusive and 10 am – 4pm November to March. *Prices:* £6 for adults, £4.50 concessions, £3 for children: tickets cover 12 months. Covered by YAT Passes. *Telephone*: 01904 610275. *Website*: **www.barleyhall.org.uk/**. *Location*: centre of Map square D3

No. 35 Stonegate, YO1 8AW. Much of the beautiful woodcarving, plasterwork and stained glass on the front was by a renowned Victorian craftsman, who lived in an elegant home behind this 15th century shop. Till mid-2014

Latticed windows of medieval house, 19 Stonegate,
now a spectacular German Christmas Shop

'Printer's Devil', street sign on former printer's
Shop in Stonegate

this supposedly haunted house was open to the public as *Haunted*, a sort of up-market indoor Ghost Walk. Change of ownership has turned it into a fashionable knick-knacks shop. In the upstairs room facing the street you can see elaborately carved wood panelling and there's some nice ceiling painting. But the shop conversion has obliterated the mystery and charm of the interior in its dimly lit *Haunted* days. No regrets though at the disappearance of *Haunted's* scariest feature – the whopping price it charged to look round the place!

CAFÉS, RESTAURANTS AND PUBS IN HISTORIC BUILDINGS

Another way to tour historic York buildings is as a customer of restaurants, cafeterias or pubs within fine old buildings like the following.

St Williams College

Address: 3 College St, York YO1 7JF, Tel. (01904) 634830
Location: behind east end of York Minster in the bottom left of Map square E2, near **Treasurer's House**.

This beautiful black and white timbered building is now usually open as a cathedral conference centre plus an all-day tea-room and restaurant – with tables outside and in its charming cobbled courtyard.

It was built in 1461 to house 24 of York's problematic 'chantry priests'. In their Wills rich men were leaving investments to fund permanent full-time employment of a 'chantry priest' simply to pray for their soul. This was such an cushy number that under-occupied chantry priests got into mischief, bringing the priesthood into disrepute. This building was intended to create a supervised, orderly home environment for them.

Sometimes you can visit the fine historic rooms upstairs. The furthest room looks into a chantry priest's small private room with original painted wall decorations. Early in the Civil War, Charles I moved the Royal Mint and his printing press to this building, since York, not London, was his base.

Black Swan Inn

Address: 23 Peaseholme Green, York, YO1 7PR. Tel. (01904) 679131

Location: Map – F3. Not marked on the map but quite near DIG.

Another beautiful black and white building, this one built in 1417 as a wealthy merchant's home. Today it's a pub, décor hardly changed since the 17th century. It's supposed to be haunted by several ghosts and a clay pipe with spooky associations is on display in the bar. Meals are often available. Frequent live folk music, including the renowned weekly Thursday evening Black Swan Folk Club, up the hilariously uneven ancient staircase. For the latter's programme: **www.blackswanfolkclub.org.uk/** or see leaflets in pub's entrance. Large car park at back.

Spurriergate Centre

Address: St Michael's Church, Spurriergate, York YO1 9QR. Tel. (01904) 629393

Location: Map – bottom of D4, where Coney St meets Low Ousegate, but not marked.

You would never guess that behind the door of this converted medieval church is a delightful snack restaurant where you eat among graceful Gothic pillars and stained glass. Under the old Ten Commandments board, there's a young children's play area with toys. It's open Monday to Friday 10 am – 4 pm Saturdays from 9.30am till 5pm. Full meals are available around lunchtime. Prices are non-tourist, for tourists don't know about this venue nor the next one.

Kings Manor

Address: Exhibition Square, York YO1 7EP
Location: Map – bottom of C2.
Places nearby: **Art Gallery**, **Yorkshire Museum**.

Today this former royal palace is part of York University and its cafeteria dining hall is open to the public for snacks and light lunches, Mondays to Fridays, 9.30 am – 3.30 pm. Walk through the grand Jacobean entrance, past the porters' lodge and, in the first courtyard, go up the stone staircase on the left of the tree. Originally this building was the lavish Abbot's house at St Mary's Abbey – the ruins in Museum Gardens. After Henry VIII's seizure of the monasteries it was enlarged as a royal palace where kings stayed and where, until 1692, the government of the north of England was based. Next it housed an exclusive girls' school, 1712 – 1835, and pupils' graffiti, celebrating their schoolgirl crushes, are carved on some window panes – by the young ladies' diamond rings.

The Grand Assembly Rooms

Address: Blake Street, York YO1 8QG, Tel. (01904) 637254
Location: On far left of Map square D3. Not marked on map but it's almost next door to the Blake St entrance to the **Visit York** tourist information office.

Today it's an Italian restaurant called ASK, but once the Assembly Rooms was a top venue for the fashionable social scene which evolved around York and its Racecourse in the 18th century. It was purpose-built in 1731-35 in the chic new Palladian style to host the balls, concerts and dinners at York which were becoming part of the Georgian gentry's social calendar. There's a grand classical portico and the interior is bounded with marble Corinthian columns.

Other historic places for food or drink

There are also cafés at the Treasurer's House and the Bar Convent, mentioned earlier. Additionally, Grays Inn Court and three cafés in towers on the City Walls are mentioned in Chapter 3.

Besides the Black Swan, other medieval pubs are:

- Snickelways Inn, 47 Goodramgate, YO1 7LS (map E3)
- Red Lion, 2 Merchantgate YO1 9TU (map E5 / F5 / top border).
- Another very old pub is the Olde Starre Inne, 40 Stonegate YO1 8AS (map D3).

For well-preserved Victorian pubs try:

- 'Golden Ball', 2 Cromwell Road YO1 6DU (D6)
- 'Phoenix', 75 George Street, YO1 9PT next to the City Walls (F6).

A particularly famous pub is the tiny, perfectly preserved, Edwardian 'Blue Bell', 53 Fossgate, YO1 9TF (E4).

Many York pubs are named after either racehorses or, like this one, public executions – because races and executions both brought crowds to pubs

York Nuclear War Observation Bunker

In a nutshell

Had nuclear war occurred, 60 RAF observers inside this suburban York bunker would have been sending 'the government' their estimates about the H bomb hell destroying Britain. Your hour-long tour of this once secret site gives a memorable picture about how government thinks about the unthinkable.

Contact details

Address: Monument Close, York YO24 4HT
English Heritage phone: 01904-646940
Website:
www.english-heritage.org.uk/daysout/properties/york-cold-war-bunker/

Location: outside Map area, see below. *Places nearby*: **Holgate Windmill**.

Getting there

Monument Close is a cul-de-sac off the B1224 (Acomb Road) in a residential York suburb within 30 minutes walk from York railway station. Since it was a secret location, some street maps still do not show Monument Close.

From Micklegate Bar, walk along Blossom Street (Map square A6), then take second turn right along Holgate Road and off the City Centre map. Continue for some distance. Then take the large left fork along Acomb Road. Walk along Acomb Road's right side past Grantham Drive, then Braeside Gardens – and the next right junction is Monument Close. English Heritage website shows detailed map.

By bus, take either the No.1 from either Theatre Royal or railway station – ask for the New Lane stop on Acomb Road. Or the No. 10 bus from either from Picadilly or railway station - ask for the Fox Pub stop, which is near the fork with Acomb Road. Then as above.

There's also a bleak short-cut which reduces the walk to 15 minutes even. Head towards the part of the Railway Museum on *the left side* of Leeman Road and take a bleak urban footpath which starts between the Museum and a car park. Follow it over a long grim footbridge across the railway tracks, then take the street straight ahead till a T-junction. Then right to the traffic lights and there's the left fork to Acomb Road.

Opening times and prices
- Open on Saturdays and Sundays for hour-long guided tours on the hour, starting at 10 am with last tour at 3 pm. No need to book tours. But check website re tour times.
- Prices: Adults £7.50. Concessions £6.80. Children £4.50. Family £19.20. Free to English Heritage members.

What it's like
In service between 1961 and 1991, the bunker reflects an era when nuclear attacks on US bases in Britain were a likely early stage of any nuclear war between US and USSR. Britain was studded with American nuclear weapon bases. The Americans' preferred attack strategy was 'limited nuclear war in Europe', whereby US bases in Britain would attack Russian bases in Eastern Europe. Thus America itself might escape devastation, unless the Russians escalated attacks to their respective homelands.

The purpose of this bunker was to analyse reports of nuclear explosions and pass on to central government. It has a mast to detect blasts in the atmosphere. It employed devices like pin-hole cameras to locate the brilliant initial flash of a nuclear explosion. Besides the location of explosions, their height would be assessed and whether the nuclear fireball had touched the ground, which produces massive radioactive fall-out.

In the central operations room, you see how in a pre-digital age a picture of our destruction could be assembled simply by putting stickers on a wall map. There are green stickers for 'air bursts', where a high altitude explosion produces greatest deaths from fire and blast. And red stickers for 'ground bursts' where it is radioactive fall-out which is the big killer. And stick-on 'fall-out plumes' to show where the wind was taking the deadly dust.

Thinking of fall-out, the bunker had its own air filtration system – along with self-contained food, water and power – so its large observer team could hole up here uninterrupted for the whole nuclear war. The staff were to be 60 Royal Observer Corps volunteers, who wore RAF uniforms. They were mainly women – often RAF wives. But 150 were recruited because of fears that, in a nuclear war, many volunteers might go sane and refuse to leave their families. Once the first 60 had arrived, the bunker's door would be locked for the duration.

Everything remains in place. You see the RAF style dormitories with iron bunks where 'hot-bedding' was practiced as shifts changed for 24 hour cover. Décor is 'Early Sixties Institutional' with plastic wherever possible, which heightens the banal feel of the bunker. Many of the secret volunteers are still in York. They say it was a hot, cramped living place on exercises.

The detailed, matter-of-fact calculations in the operations room contrast strangely with the likely horrors outside the bunker. Could central government in its own deep bunker really have used this information constructively, one wonders. Or were these bunkers just helping governments to imagine that they could enter a nuclear war and still somehow stay in charge, just by keeping tabs on things through places like this?

Holgate Windmill

In a nutshell
A beautiful five-sailed restored windmill, where you can climb to the top and learn interesting things about how windmills are run.

Contact details
Address: Holgate Windmill, Windmill Rise, York YO26 4TX
Phone: 01904 799295 (project secretary)
Website: **www.holgatewindmill.org**
Location: outside Map area, see below. *Places nearby*: **Nuclear War Observation Bunker**.

Getting there
Follow the same walk or bus directions as for the nearby Nuclear War Observation Bunker as far as the left fork along Acomb Road and start to walk along Acomb Road's right side. But before you reach any side road, look for a bus stop beside a sign '68-70 Acomb Road' and take the lane there, which leads quickly to the Windmill. (Bus stop and lane are directly opposite the side road, New Lane)

Opening times and prices
- Between May and the end of October usually open on Saturdays, Sundays and Bank Holidays 11 am – 4 pm. During other months tends to be open Saturdays only, 10 am – 12 pm, for flour sales. Check with website.
- Prices: Adults £3. Young people (6 -18) £1.

What it's like

This unusual and beautiful five-sailed windmill was built in 1770 and operated commercially right up to 1933, one of the last windmills in Britain. Restoration of the huge sails and the corn-grinding stones was completed during 2012. Corn milling is beginning but wind operation is not yet routine. You can climb up three floors and see the mechanism at the very top. Friendly volunteers explain things like:

- The different types of mill stone which the mill uses and the various grains on display.

- The wind-powered fantail mechanism which turns the top of the windmill so the sails always face the wind.
- How the shutters on the sails open or close to increase or decrease the wind's impact.
- Tales of the various millers who used to run this mill – and of York's many other windmills, now vanished.
- Hazards of the miller's life like flour dust explosions, lung disease, and very strong winds.

NB Upper floors are reached by steep, ladder-like stairs.

Riverside and Racecourse History Walk

In a nutshell

A leafy contrast to the city, a 30 minute riverside walk along a Georgian posers' parade leads to York's new Millenium Bridge, where you can picnic on seats above mid-river. Afterwards there's an optional long route back across York's vast Knavesmire Racecourse, past the old gallows site. Nearby is chocolate magnate Terry's pleasant private garden, now open via the National Trust.

So the walk embraces three of York's traditional moneyspinners – the racecourse, chocolate manufacture and big, festive public hangings.

Starting point

You can start from anywhere on the riverside path heading downstream from Ouse Bridge on the Minster / Castle Museum side of the Ouse. Walk downstream along the Ouse to Skeldergate Bridge – there's a quaint tower with café seating outside it. Continue under the arch on the immediate left of this tower. You are now in New Walk, an avenue of horse chestnuts, maples, and limes – on the Map it's square E6.

'The New Walk'

This riverside avenue walk was created in the 1730s as a stylish promenading place where fashion-conscious folk could stroll and pose, see and be seen. It belongs to the same Georgian York social scene as Fairfax House, the Assembly Rooms, the Racecourse and Beningbrough Hall. York's Art Gallery holds 18th century paintings of posers on parade in New Walk.

On your right is the Ouse. On your left is a car park, which used to be a duelling grounds, St George's Fields. Continue along the avenue, crossing a blue bridge over the Foss tributary, which joins the Ouse. There's a view to the left of the Foss floodgates. During the December 2015 floods, these failed dramatically owing to government spending cuts to their maintenance. Continue along the avenue alongside the Ouse. Soon you'll see something like a small Sydney Harbour Bridge – it's Millenium Bridge, your destination.

Just after a sign to Hartoft Street, on your left is Pikeing Well and on your right an information board about this 18th century medicinal well. Its waters were used for sore eyes but its dank, sludgy interior is nowadays more like an eye sore. The Well's 'health' image took a knock in the 1920s when it transpired that it was fed by a stream which filtered through York Cemetery. Pikeing Well is the very first building designed by John Carr. From its blank, no frills design, you'd never guess that he'd later become the famous, fashionable architect who created Harewood House, Fairfax House, York Law Courts and much else in Yorkshire. Carr received £88 for designing Pikeing Well. For the artistic effort involved, even at today's prices this looks quite generous.

Closer to Millenium Bridge you may notice a narrow gauge railtrack leading from the river bank. This once transferred gunpowder from boats from London's Woolwich armoury which supplied the army depot next to the Ouse. Before the railway, the swiftest York-London route was by boat down the Ouse and into the River Humber, then via the North Sea to reach London via the Thames estuary. The wharves and warehouses near where you start this walk are mementoes of York's centuries as an inland port.

You'll reach the Millenium Bridge, no more than 30 minutes after starting. There are picnic benches on the bank. But the best seats are the broad benches on the bridge itself, which let you lean back over the dark green waters of the Ouse. Swallows dart and occasional boats pass underneath. In autumn there are wonderful leaf colours from the tall trees. Downstream, on the far bank is the clock tower of the famous Terry's Chocolate Factory.

There's a choice of routes back.

Quick route back on the other side of the Ouse
Cross Millenium Bridge, turn right and walk back along the Ouse on the other bank. The fine avenue here is part of Rowntrees Park, given to York by its other great chocolate manufacturer, Joseph Rowntree. It is one of many good things which this generous Quaker family gave to York. You end up on the side of Skeldergate Bridge opposite to where you started.

Long route back via Knavesmire racecourse
For a longer route back, cross Millenium Bridge, turn left and follow the path along the Ouse downstream until the cycle track turns sharply right and leads you to the main road. Cross this road and turn left in front of the former Terry's chocolate factory. See how the tower's clockface has 'Terrys of York' in place of numerals.

Very soon, take a path rightwards towards the Racecourse. The latter developed in the 18th century as a major entertainment for fashionable Georgian folk. You may walk across the Racecourse as long as not a race day. Look for the little gates through the railings guarding the main racetrack. From the centre, the Racecourse can feel splendidly vast.

Incorporated within today's large stands is the original 1754 luxury classical grandstand. This replaced watching racing, while sitting in your carriage. To get in, you had to buy a 100 year timeshare, which fitted the snobbery of Georgian York's racing scene.

Today York can get very festive around big races. For dates, see:**www.yorkracecourse.co.uk/racing/** . The unusual names of many pubs in York often come from famous racehorses here.

It takes 10 minutes from Millenium Bridge to the edge of the Racecourse, then 15 minutes to cross Knavesmire Racecourse towards busy Tadcaster Road.

Once on Tadcaster Road, a rightwards turn would lead you towards the Micklegate Bar gateway in York's City Walls.

The old gallows site
On the edge of the Racecourse on Tadcaster Road is a former gallows site where, 1379 – 1801, huge numbers of people were slowly hanged before a gawping public. Nicknamed the 'Three-Legged Mare', a three-sided gallows enabled multiple hangings. In 1739, highwayman Dick Turpin met his end here. Hangings and horse-racing sometimes took place in sight of each other.

Look for a little paved area with two benches, a stone marker and an information board. It's on the edge of

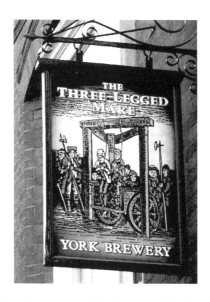

A York pub sign shows the Knavesmire's three-sided gallows

Tadcaster Road almost opposite Pulleyn Drive, on the out-of-town side of Tadcaster Road's junction with Knavesmire Road. Here were hanged many political prisoners through centuries of rebellions, plus many people guilty of thoroughly petty crimes and plenty who were probably not guilty of anything. If anywhere should be haunted….

A chocolate magnate's garden: Goddards
If wishing further greenery, once on Tadcaster Road, head left and look for No. 27. This is Goddards, the former home of the Terry family, whose chocolate factory you passed earlier. Nowadays it's a National Trust HQ and for a small fee (Trust members free) you can enjoy its large gardens, tour the Arts and Crafts Movement house or enjoy lunch or tea in a well-cultivated 1930s ambience. The garden is Edwardian in style with a pool inspired by Indian Mughal gardens. The best bit is at the very back, a shady natural

water garden with green pools and a rockery of mossy, eroded limestone rocks from the Dales.

Goddards

Address: Goddards, 27 Tadcaster Road, York YO24 1GG
Telephone: 01904-771-930
Website: **www.nationaltrust.org.uk/goddards/**

Opening times and prices
- March – October, Wednesday – Sunday inclusive, 10.30 am – 5 pm.

- Adult £6.90. Child £3.40. Family £17.20.

Arts and Crafts era elegance at the Terrys' home, Goddards

Beningbrough Hall

In a nutshell
National Trust Georgian stately home with pleasant garden and restaurant, 10 miles north-west from York and easily reached by bus or bike. A large, clever exhibition of 18th century portraits with child-friendly input about the portrait painter's trade. Quite amazing how they've attuned this to children! A creative style of stewardship pervades this place.

Contact details
Address: Beningbrough Hall, York, North Yorkshire YO30 1DD
Telephone: 01904-472027
Website:
www.nationaltrust.org.uk/beningbrough-hall-gallery-and-gardens

Opening times, and prices
In January, February, November and December, the galleries, gardens and restaurant only are open at weekends, 11.30 am – 3.30 pm.
- During school half-terms, and from March to June and in September and October, everything is open, House included, every day except Monday.
- In July and August everything is open seven days a week.
- Opening hours are usually 12 pm – 5 pm for the House and 10.30 am – 5 pm for the Gardens.
- On Bank Holiday Mondays, everything is open.
It is a complicated pattern, so check by phone or website.

Prices
- When the whole property is open: Adults £12.50. Children £6.25. Family tickets £31.25.

- For winter months' partial openings, Adults £7.20. Children £3.60. Family tickets £18
- National Trust members enter free.

Visitors on bicycles sometimes get reductions.

Facilities

- Nice all-day restaurant and café with indoor and outdoor sections.
- Children's adventure playground in a woodland corner.
- Nearby farm shop.
- Many special events – see website.

Getting there

Take the No.29 bus from near York Art Gallery to the Village Hall stop at Newton-on-Ouse. The bus ride takes 25 minutes. From the bus stop, walk briefly in same direction, then take first left turn past pretty houses and in 10 minutes you'll reach the gates to Beningbrough Hall. Then it's 15 minutes further walk along the avenue to the Hall. You need to plan the trip, since buses run only every two hours or so and the last bus back may leave Newton-on-Ouse at 6 pm.

For bus information, see YorkshireTravel.Net.

A cycle track runs all the way from near York's Museum Gardens. See cycle map:
www.york.gov.uk/content/45053/64877/64891/York_cycle _route_map.pdf

A footpath runs along the River Ouse between Beningbrough Hall and Museum Gardens. A 10 mile, three hour walk through grasslands, so surely one way only. And that one way should be back from Beningbrough, lest you miss the turn off from the river to the Hall.

For footpath or cycle path, you can ask for Beningbrough Hall's own simple map showing the start point back to York.

What it's like
It's a classical early 18th century Hall in brick. It was built by a young heir who, enthused by his Grand Tour, raced home to tear down his Elizabethan ancestral mansion and replace it with this louder Baroque fashion statement.

Everything is smartly rectangular and there's a dramatically high entrance hall to awe visitors.

Furnishings-wise, look out for:

- Rare, immensely tall, Queen Anne period four-poster beds with elaborate roofs – great status symbols at the time.
- The 18th century vogue for Chinese furniture – screens with stories illustrated in panels, a pretty little Chinese writing cabinet, and Chinese vases.
- Fabulous woodwork on the ground floor at the back.

The portrait displays
The National Portrait Gallery has loaned 100 eighteenth century portraits. These are cleverly used in ways which can engage both adults and children.

For some portraits you can learn more by pressing their number on the audio-guide – like tales of a vicious serial duellist, or of the 'Kit Kat Club', a cabal of scheming, rich, young, Queen Anne era politicians. One section gets children to study how painters slyly slipped hints and messages into portraits – complete with task sheets.

Beningbrough Hall

Children can dress up for an 18th century portrait, choose props to project a personal image, and pose in front of a gilt framed mirror.

They can draw portraits too. If you can't draw, there's computer-assisted portrait making.

Budding sculptors can style a new plasticene nose for a bust of Captain Cook.

Look out for the portrait of an 18th century fashion commentator. His daughter is trying to draw his attention, showing a doll with an absurd high fashion hairstyle.

In the same room, another portrait shows a bling 18th century family posing with such fashionable trinkets that the gods in the sky are looking sour with envy. One cherub has even sneaked down to earth for a party bag from such wealthy mortals.

The garden

In a large walled garden, fruit and vegetables are grown in traditional arrangements which are picturesque in themselves. There are beautiful old glass cloches, arches made from pleached pear trees, huge pumpkins and sunflowers and espaliered apple trees. There's a curious collection of historic lawnmowers, a fabulous giant teapot sculpture and many nice places to sit.

Giant teapot in Beningbrough Hall's outdoor café

York City Walls on their high grassy banks

*The walkway along the Walls' battlements means you can
walk round the City*

CHAPTER THREE

WALKING YORK'S CITY WALLS:
A DETAILED GUIDE

What's in this chapter
The grandest in Britain, York's City Walls are between two and three miles long and are almost completely preserved. They look their very best in April when thousands of daffodils bloom on their grassy banks.

This chapter guides you the whole way round on their battlements. Or you can choose short sections which take around 15 minutes each, for there are many stairs where you can climb on or off the Walls.

Close to these stairs, often there are interesting information boards. Information given here largely complements, rather than duplicates, the latter.

The route described here includes the following extras to the standard 'York Walls Walk':

- two museums in towers on the Wall, the **Richard III Museum** and **Micklegate Bar Museum**, and a café in a third tower, **Walmgate Bar** .
- detour to the **grave of highwayman Dick Turpin**.
- **Cliffords Tower**, the old castle's Keep, infamous for the 12th century massacre of York's Jews.
- The Roman fortress '**Multangular Tower**' in Museums Gardens.
- It starts with the section which is many people's favourite, **Bootham Bar to Monk Bar**.

Planning your walk

- Allow between two and three hours for the route described here - not including detours, like the museums in the towers.
- Know in advance when the Walls close - from 9.00 pm mid-summer to 3.30 pm in winter. Usually the little gates to the walls carry signs – often 'closes at dusk'.
- Picturesque cafés are mentioned near the first, fourth and seventh sections of this walk. There are toilets near the sixth section and near Bootham Bar, this walk's start and finish point.

Bootham Bar and history of York's City Walls

Bootham Bar is the gate opposite the Art Gallery on the right of Map square C2. Before climbing the steps up the Wall, notice the portcullis in the gate tower's round outer arch next to the road. The roundness of the arch shows it is late 11th or early 12th century. But the tower's upper part is 14th century.

York's Walls are a patchwork from different periods. They were largely built during the 13th and 14th centuries. But they incorporate parts of York's much smaller Roman fortress and there are also 17th and 18th century modifications and a chunk of 19th century restoration.

Bootham Bar faces the road from Scotland and its gate had a huge oak knocker with which Scottish people were required to knock for permission to enter York. This makes symbolic sense because wars with Scotland were a prime reason for York's walls being rebuilt in stone in the early 13th century.

- These strong city walls gave the King of England a powerbase in the north.

- They made York a secure place where an army could gradually assemble for a war with Scotland or against a northern rebellion and where weapons and siege machinery could be stored.
- For a long war in the north, the Walls made York a safe place where the King could conduct government and the war simultaneously, like a northern capital. During their Scottish wars, Edward I started holding parliaments in York (in the Minster's Chapter House) and moved his treasure there, while Edward III brought the whole royal family as well.
- If a war went badly, York's Walls meant you could flee back and slam the gate shut, as Edward II did in 1314 after defeat by the Scots at Bannockburn.

York's Walls also created a secure place where royal enemies could be imprisoned, then publicly executed and their heads stuck above the gates. High profile executions became quite an industry for York. Several pub signs commemorate this - like the Three Legged Mare, on the left pavement of High Petergate as you face Bootham Bar. 'Three Legged Mare' was a nickname for the gallows.

York's Walls primarily served royal power, not York citizens, and their history is full of citizens' complaints about paying for them.

Could York's City Walls keep attackers out?
The Walls themselves proved very effective at deterring attack. But their human operators sometimes let the side down.

Scottish raiders repeatedly avoided attacking York. But English rebellions proved a tricky matter. The 14th and 15th centuries were full of coup attempts by minor royals, some of which succeeded. Today's treasonable rebel could become tomorrow's rightful king - like Henry IV, Edward IV or Henry VII. So York's civic leaders would bob and weave to avoid being on the losing side. While some rebels found the gates shut, others were let in with excuses.

When the deposed Edward IV tried a comeback and demanded entry to York for his army, the City hedged its bets. He was allowed in for one night only. Lucky, because he later retook the Crown.

When 20,000 Catholic rebels advanced on York in 1536, the City adopted a ruse. A letter was sent to Henry VIII requesting urgent reinforcements to resist them. Two days later, surprise, surprise, no royal troops had arrived. So York's Council had to open the gates to the rebels, hadn't they? And to act responsibly and protect property, shouldn't they first negotiate the best deal obtainable from the rebels? Which turned out to be that only royal property would be stolen. Amazingly, after Henry VIII regained control, York got away with this.

The only time York's Walls were properly tested was the fierce three month Civil War siege during 1644, when York was a key Royalist base. Twice Parliament's troops penetrated the Walls – at Walmgate Bar and near today's Museum Gardens – but they were driven out again. A Royalist army arrived to relieve York and Parliament's troops gave up their siege.

But then York's Royalist garrison made a terrible mistake. They joined up with the Royalist relief army and left York to chase the retreating Parliamentary army. At Marston Moor, near York, these Royalists were massively defeated. Parliament's troops then headed back to York, which surrendered swiftly since it now lacked sufficient defenders.

York's City Walls with their famous daffodils

Re-enactment on York's racecourse of the battle of Marston Moor (1644) which forced the surrender of York

Section 1: Bootham Bar to Monk Bar

In Bootham Bar's tower, you can see the portcullis close-up before you step out along on the battlements. Soon you get a view of the dry moat along the outside of the Wall. In medieval times this ditch was filled with water diverted from the River Foss, which this walk later passes. Looking inwards are wonderful views towards the Minster which make this section of the Walls Walk many people's favourite. (Mapwise you are in Map squares D2 & E2)

Soon, look out for a staircase downwards on your right, signed for Grays Court Tea Room and Garden. This is a pleasant place for food or drink – details of this historic building on: **grayscourtyork.com/index.php**
Continuing along the Wall till Monk Bar tower – this section takes around 15 minutes. Your choices now are:

- Turn right down the dark flight of steps in the Monk Bar tower and cross Goodramgate street then climb back on to the Walls on the other side of the tower.
- First visit the museum in Monk Bar's tower.

Detour to **Monk Bar Richard III Museum**

The building
Inside this medieval gatehouse tower you can see:

- The mechanism for operating the portcullis.
- In a tiny turret, a prison cell with an authentic medieval toilet, which emptied straight down from the tower wall.
- Another cramped prison cell which tells the tale of Alice Bowman, a prisoner of conscience gaoled there in Elizabeth I's reign. She had removed the head of a Catholic which had been publicly displayed on a spike.

Bootham Bar, the gate to the road to Scotland.
The round arch is from the Norman period.

View from the Walls towards the Minster in the background. In the foreground is Gray's Court Tea Garden which you can enter directly down steps from the Walls.

The City Walls near Monkgate Bar

New exhibition about Richard III

Since 2014, the tower hosts a new look exhibition about Richard III and battles of the 15th century Wars of the Roses.

- A suit of armour plus replica medieval helmets. Parents, you may help your children to hoist the hefty helmets on to their heads. Officially sanctioned!
- Text panels tell of Richard III's rumoured murders of his nephews and wife, death in battle in 1485, and reappearance under a Leicester car park in 2013.
- For adults, a sombre video about the 1461 Battle of Towton - 28,000 slaughtered in the snow, shattered skulls now uncovered from mass graves etc.
- Children get a Fast Forward video about the same – in spritely Horrible Histories style, while seated in a snug tent.

Contact details

Address: Richard III Experience, Monk Bar, York, YO1 7LQ
Phone: 01904-615505
Website: **http://richardiiiexperience.com**

Location: Map – E2.

Opening times and prices

- Open daily. April - October, 10 am – 5 pm. November to March 10 am – 4 pm,.
- Admission charges: adult £5, concessions £3.50, child £3. Family tickets & combination tickets with other attractions.
- Tickets provide entry to both this tower museum and to the Henry VII museum at **Micklegate Bar** and can be used repeatedly for 12 months.

Section 2: Monk Bar to Foss Islands Road

It's worth looking at the picturesque exterior of Monk Bar before you climb back on to the Wall by the stairs on the other side of the road.

Once back on the Walls, soon there's a flight of seven steps and a snowflake symbol on the battlements' pavement. Here look outwards and beneath the walls there's something like a brick igloo. It's an early 19th century ice storage house. Here, well shaded on the north of the City Wall, ice from the frozen Ouse was stored for use later in the year. From Monkgate there's easy access to this ice house through a pub car park. You can peer down into a deep pit inside it.

Beside the snowflake symbol, look inwards from the battlement and below you'll see the uncovered foundations of a tower from the Roman fortress. A moment later, there's a good information board about another Roman tower. You are at a corner of the Roman fortress.

Next, looking inwards, the old Hall of the Merchant Taylors Guild is visible close to the Wall. On the Walls' battlements, opposite the Hall's far end, there are two arched niches. These are said to be remains from medieval lavatories, which discharged outside the Walls. This section takes perhaps 10 minutes.

Section 3: Foss Islands Road to the Red Tower

This part of medieval York's defences never needed any walls because it was a mix of a large royal fish farm and impassable swamp. William the Conqueror began a massive engineering project which dammed and diverted the River Foss before it reached the Ouse. First it flowed into the huge King's Pool, where people paid steeply to fish bream and pike as a royal income generator - William was extremely money-minded. Then the river formed a water moat outside the City Walls, flowing down to the Ouse and around the Castle's Keep. Finally it powered a water mill before joining the larger River Ouse – more income generation. All this has gone. The King's Pool has largely silted up and you see the River Foss flowing a different route today.

To reach the next section of Walls, turn slightly right as you leave the previous section. Cross the road, then cross the waterway immediately to your left, the River Foss. Then continue walking with the River Foss on your right and a busy road on your left. This was all once the King's Pool. It's Map square G3.

When the River Foss curves off to your right, don't follow it: stick to the pavement along the big road. After a builder's yard and some houses you reach the Red Tower and the Walls again, just five minutes after you left them.

Section 4: Red Tower to Walmgate Bar

The Red Tower was a 1490 reinforcement by Henry VII to deal with local uprisings against his heavy taxes. He built it in brick, unlike the rest of the Walls, which led to a murderous conflict between stonemasons and bricklayers, as the information board describes.

Climbing back on the Walls, you'll notice they are much lower than earlier in your walk. In 1745 this section was deliberately reduced in height and loopholed for muskets. This was in preparation for Bonnie Prince Charlie's Scottish Highlanders who were invading England - though in the event they bypassed York. Earlier, during the lead-up to the Civil War of 1642-1646, some other parts of the Walls were likewise lowered so as better to resist cannon fire. Lower walls offered less of a target and made it harder for a cannon ball to destroy long stretches of parapet. This section takes five minutes.

Walmgate Bar and the café inside

Walmgate Bar is a large gate tower – bottom right corner of Map square G5. It saw the fiercest fighting of the intense three month siege in 1644. Parliament's troops dug a secret tunnel under Walmgate Bar, packed with gunpowder to blow it up. But the Royalists discovered this from a prisoner and dug a tunnel of their own to flood it.

You can see bullet marks from the siege if you go through the arch into the barbican, then turn round and look at the right hand turret on the gatehouse itself. As at other gates, there's a rounded arch from Norman times. But much of it is later, like the pretty Elizabethan structure on the city side with its classical pilasters and latticed windows. This used to be rented out as housing – income generation was a pressing issue for these City Walls, where King and York residents constantly argued about maintenance costs.

Today Walmgate Bar contains a pleasant, atmospheric café. Its top floor hasn't changed greatly from Civil War days, apart from no Roundheads trying to get in. If you ask, café staff may let you walk out on the walls of the barbican. From here you can see the bullet marks on the turret especially clearly. At street level outside, before the next steps up to the Walls, there's an information board which explains the barbican's purpose.

Section 5: Walmgate to Fishergate Bar

It takes five minutes to reach Fishergate Bar, a small gate (Map square F6) Here you need briefly to come down from the Wall. Then there's an information board about Fishergate Bar's turbulent history. But before you go back up on the Wall, you could take a couple of minutes to visit the grave of the famous highwayman, Dick Turpin, who was hanged at York in 1739.

Elegant structure on the inside of Walmgate Bar.
*Nowadays there's a **café** inside.*

Cliffords Tower, the surviving Keep of York Castle on the grassy mound where William the Conqueror built his original wooden castle.

Surviving outer curtain walls of York Castle, now within the Castle Museum.

Quick detour to **Dick Turpin's grave**
Head briefly rightwards, inwards from the City Walls, cross
Lead Mill Lane (Map square F6) and take the first gate on
your left into a little graveyard. The wages of crime, it
seems, are an easy-to-spot grave. Its massive bulk reflects
fear of 'bodysnatchers' seeking to steal his corpse.

Section 6: Fishergate to Cliffords Tower
Back on the Walls, it takes perhaps five minutes to
Fishergate Postern, a 16th century tower which ends the
Walls Walk till after you cross the River Ouse. This roomy,
four storey tower is at present usually closed but it may
open with a café and a small museum about the City Walls.
Once it guarded a pedestrians' entrance to York. By
Georgian times it was being rented out as an exotic party
venue in the quest to milk money from the City Walls.

Descending from the Walls, you must next cross the River
Foss by the bridge which you'll see in front of you. Toilets
are nearby in St George's Fields Car Park on the left side of
the road. Otherwise stay on the right side and follow the
pavement round to the right. On the map, this is E6.

The medieval castle and the 18th century prisons
In medieval times the area on your right was guarded by
York Castle and the River Foss was channelled to create a
moat in front of the Castle's walls. Almost all that now
remains of York Castle is its Keep, Cliffords Tower.

Demolition of the rest was begun by Richard III, a Yorkist,
who was intending to replace it with an even grander castle.
But in 1485 he was overthrown by Lancastrian Henry VII,
who naturally halted his rival's project.

The decaying Castle was damaged in the 1644 Civil War
siege. Then under Charles II it was partly used as a prison
– for Quakers in particular, up to 500 at a time.

The changing face of York Castle

Model of York Castle in medieval times. On left, surrounded by a moat, is its Keep, Cliffords Tower, which survives today.

Cliffords Tower, the surviving Castle Keep, today

View from Cliffords Tower towards the 18th century 'Law & Order complex' which replaced the rest of the Castle. On right is the Law Courts. Central & left buildings were prisons, now the Castle Museum.

Then steadily much Castle building was demolished to make way for two 18th century prisons and a Law Court. It is these 18th century prison buildings which you now see on your right. Highwayman Dick Turpin was imprisoned here before his execution. A succession of late 18th and early 19th century political prisoners were jailed here, like the poet journalist James Montgomery and the Chartists Samuel Holberry and Feargus O'Connor.

Follow the pavement round to the right (Map square E5) till you see the surviving Keep, Cliffords Tower, on a steep grassy mound. To your right is the 18th century Law and Order complex. The right hand building is still a Law Court. The other two buildings, the two former prisons, are now the vast **Castle Museum** of bygone English lifestyle, where some former cells are preserved, as described in the next chapter.

Doorway for the doomed
At the near end of the former prison opposite the Law Court, behind some birch trees there's a faint former doorway, strangely high above ground and now filled with a latticed window. Quite recently this led on to a gallows platform. This was for the new, discreet, late Victorian, Not-In-Front-Of-The-Children sort of execution, since the present car park was then a walled prison yard.

Cliffords Tower: the Castle Keep, YO1 9SA

Cliffords Tower was begun by William the Conqueror as a wooden tower on a mound – a primitive 'motte and bailey' castle.

This was burned down during the infamous massacre of York's large Jewish community in 1190. There's a memorial near the steps up to Cliffords Tower. The story of the massacre is as follows.

The 1190 massacre of the Jews of York

It seems likely that the massacre resulted from a cold-blooded criminal plot by some local minor noblemen. They had borrowed from York's Jewish bankers to fund extravagant lifestyles and now plotted to evade their debts.

In March 1190 a mysterious gang raided the house of a prominent Jewish family, murdered the occupants, stole their property and set the house on fire. The next day most of York's Jewish community fled to the King's wooden castle where today's Clifford's Tower stands. They were granted protection there, as entitled, by the castle's officer-in-charge, a royal appointee.

Further attacks then took place on Jews remaining outside the castle. The Jews inside began to fear that the castle's royal officers might hand them over to their enemies outside – a sadly plausible scenario. So the Jews took over the little wooden castle and locked the King's officers out.

At this, the castle's officer-in-charge called up local royal military reservists to retake the castle. A large mob of young men joined them, claiming this signalled royal approval for an attack. For some days the Jews defended the castle successfully. But, when siege machines were brought from York's royal military stores, they despaired.

The Rabbi called for a mass-suicide and many of the Jews followed this, after setting the wooden castle on fire. Some Jews, who had survived the fire, agreed with the besiegers to convert to Christianity so their lives would be spared. But, as they left the castle, they were all murdered anyway. Around 150 Jews died.

Immediately after the massacre, certain leading besiegers rushed to York Minster to burn the records held there of their own debts to the Jews. This suggests the true motives behind the crime. The King, Richard the Lionheart, made moves to punish the perpetrators. But it was claimed that they had fled or could not be identified. Instead, all York's wealthiest citizens received a heavy collective fine. This may have done more for the royal coffers than for justice.

Later history of Cliffords Tower
Cliffords Tower was rebuilt in stone between 1245 and 1315. It was completely surrounded by water channelled from the River Foss, a sort of inner moat inside the Castle, and was reached by a drawbridge. It was the safest place in York, where the King stored the royal treasury while up north to direct a war. In 1665 the Quaker founder George Fox was imprisoned here for two days en route for jail in Scarborough. Then the Tower was burned to a ruined shell after a mysterious gunpowder accident late 17th century.

Visiting Cliffords Tower
Before continuing the City Walls walk across the River Ouse, you could visit Cliffords Tower. It is managed by English Heritage and open daily except Christmas and New Year – usually 10 am till 6 pm in summer, closing at 4 pm in colder months. (2018 prices: Adults £5. Seniors £4.50. Children £3. Family £13. Phone: 0870-3331181.)
It is in Map square E5, YO1 9SA.

The 17th century fire reduced this two-storey, roofed Keep to a walled open courtyard with a deep well.
- You can walk all the way round the high battlements for some grand views and photo-shots – like this book's cover!
- Half-way up the tower is a tiny ruined chapel.
- Sometimes in the courtyard there's an informative model of the whole original medieval York Castle, showing the moat system.
- A shop sells child-friendly historical knick-knacks like plastic swords and armour.

Section 7: Baile Hill to Micklegate Bar - 'Mason's Marks' and the chess board

Across the Ouse lies what's probably the second prettiest stretch of York's Walls Walk. Look left from Cliffords Tower and take the pedestrian crossing over the road, turn left along the pavement, then right - across Skeldergate Bridge over the Ouse. Immediately before you cross the river, on your right is a little tower which often is open as a café. In medieval times, around here a heavy chain could be raised across the river to stop hostile ships sailing up the Ouse.

Once across the bridge, cross a side road and look for an archway into a little tower facing you. (On the Map, square D6.)

There are three little flights of steps up to the Walls. Just before the third flight, look for a star carved into the lowest stone in the wall on your right. This is a rare medieval 'Mason's Mark' and you may spot others. Probably these were how a new mason signed a sample of his work for inspection by a master mason. Such symbols became re-used in Freemasonry.

A grassy, wooded mound is next to the steps. This is Baile Hill, where another of William the Conqueror's wooden castles stood. Later, it became a platform for the Royalist defenders' heavy cannon during the 1644 siege.

Some way further on is a stone paving slab carved with a chess board. It is said that this arrived during 19th century repairs, coming from the old Castle prison, carved there by prisoners for entertainment in their cell. This is how to find it. Look ahead for the next archway through the Walls – Victoria Bar, a 19th century roadway. When you reach the little tower just before Victoria Bar, walk seven slabs back towards Baile Hill. On the eighth slab is the chess board.

After perhaps 15 minutes, you reach Micklegate Bar, York's grandest gate tower, the one facing London, where Kings ceremonially entered York. On the Map this is in square B5.

The lower parts are 12th century, the upper parts 14th century. If you briefly descend from the Walls, you can see the beautifully coloured heraldic emblems on its outside.

Not so pretty in its heyday, though, for atop Micklegate Bar, impaled on poles, would be many severed heads of people who had displeased the King. A severed head often stayed there for years, though sometimes sympathisers secretly removed them. The last date that human heads were displayed on Micklegate Bar was a dark night in January 1754. They were the heads of two executed officers from Bonnie Prince Charlie's army, impaled since 1745. These heads then mysteriously disappeared overnight. An investigation was ordered by George II and a York tailor was imprisoned for four years.

Detour to **Micklegate Bar Museum / 'Henry VII Experience'**

Address: Micklegate Bar Museum, Micklegate Bar, York YO1 6JX.
Phone: 01904-615505
Website: : **http://richardiiiexperience.com**

Opening times and prices
- Open daily. April – October: 10 am – 4 pm. November – March 10 am – 3 pm.
- Admission charges: adult £5, concessions £3.50, child £3. Family tickets & combination tickets with other attractions.

Tickets provide entry to both this tower museum and to the Richard III museum at **Monkgate Bar** and do so for 12 months.

*Micklegate Bar, the gate where kings entered York
and the heads of kings' enemies were spiked on the
battlements*

Location: Map – B5.
Places nearby: **Bar Convent**.

The building
This medieval gatehouse tower was York's prime display point for the severed heads of the most important enemies of the king. In a turret on the top floor is a moderately gruesome wax recreation of the head of a Duke of York, which was spiked here during the Wars of the Roses.

Exhibition on Henry VII
Henry VII was the final victor in the Wars of the Roses. On the tower's lower floor are text boards about life in York during his reign, including a display of herbs and spices used for medical purposes at the time. On the top floor are tales about the king himself plus children's activities:

- In a little tent, a very entertaining 'Horrible Histories' video about Henry's dealings with fraudulent claimants to the throne, plus a right royal rap to a rock tune.

- Design, crayon and cut out your own coat-of-arms on the cardboard templates provided.

- Toy sword, shield and dressing up gear for a 15th century selfie.

- Some serious replica helmets in a turret. You wouldn't know unless you ask, but parents are authorised to try these out on their children.

Section 8: Micklegate Bar to Lendal Bridge

This section of the Walls Walk takes 15 minutes. As you pass the Rail Station, there's an excellent photo opportunity towards the Minster.

Before you leave the Wall at Lendal Bridge, be sure to read the interesting information board about Barker Tower, from which a chain across the river could stop unauthorised boats. Pretty little Barker Tower is just on the left of Lendal Bridge and is sometimes open as a café.

Barker Tower, guarding the upstream river entrance to York

Section 9: the Roman 'Multangular Tower' and the Roman coffins

You can't walk any further atop the Walls. But, once over Lendal Bridge, follow the Walls on your left, then turn left into Museum Gardens – Map square C3. Keep walking and the Walls will now be on your right. Soon you see a tower with a polygonal shape.

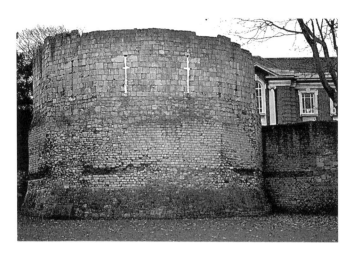

The 'Multangular Tower' in Museum Gardens. The lower section with the smaller stones was part of the Roman legionary fortress. The layer of larger blocks above is medieval.

The lower two-thirds is built with much smaller stone blocks than the top third. This lower part of the tower and the adjoining wall is the corner of the actual Roman fortress, which in medieval times was heightened and incorporated into the City Walls.

If you turn right and right again through an archway, you can reach the inside of the Multangular Tower, as this Roman tower is known. It was one of eight such Roman towers, dating at least from the reign of Constantine (306 - 337 CE). From the inside, there's a good view of this awesomely large and well-preserved chunk of Roman fortress. There is a helpful information board. Nearby are some massive stone coffins. These are also Roman and were brought here when a Roman cemetery was discovered during the building of York's rail station.

If you're interested, from inside the Multangular Tower you can continue a short distance further along the City Wall to reach the Anglian Tower, a small ruined tower built soon after the Romans departure – a rare piece of Anglo-Saxon building. Nearby is a layered bank where archaeologists have marked the ground levels for different historical periods.

Otherwise you can head back outside the Multangular Tower, turn right and follow the City Wall for a short distance to where a section was demolished in the 1820s to make way for a road. You look across to Bootham Bar where the City Wall restarts. You have come full circle.

A turret on Monkgate Bar

CHAPTER FOUR
THE MUSEUMS OF YORK

Central York

Just outside York

National Railway Museum

In a nutshell
'Not just about trains' is a catchphrase at the NRM, which has sought ways to interest everyone - from children of all ages to adult railway enthusiasts and adults with no interest in trains at all. This free entry museum is very varied and very customer-oriented – especially to families with children. Giant locomotives, luxurious royal train carriages, interactive signal box games….

Contact details
Address: NRM York, Leeman Road, York YO26 4XJ
Phone: 08448 153139
Website: **www.nrm.org.uk/**

Location: Map – A3 & 4. The Museum is on both sides of the road. Main entrance is on the far side from nearby York Rail Station.

Opening Times, Admission & Facilities
- Daily, all year, from 10 am - 5 pm, but closed from Christmas Eve to Boxing Day.
- Admission is free.
- Ample refreshment facilities.

Planning your visit
- Afternoons and weekends are generally the best times for the short talks, tours and demonstrations of machines in action.
- Check times of these in advance on NRM website or phone.
- On arriving, ask what talks & demonstrations are scheduled.

Stephenson's 1829 'Rocket' locomotive (replica)

The Great Hall

Here are more than 30 locomotives - from early 19th century prototypes to the 1960s Japanese bullet train. They come in every size, from a gigantic Chinese train to a tiny mountain locomotive. Exhibits include:

- The story of the first, very slow steam locomotives up to Stephenson's 1829 breakthrough with his speedy 'Rocket'. A snazzy yellow and black replica of the latter is on display.
- Travelling postal sorting offices explained. In a participative exhibit, children can race each other to slip letters through the right sorting slots.
- The 130 mph 'Shinkansen' Japanese 'bullet train'.
- An under-floor passage gives the experience of actually walking under one of the huge locomotives.
- Cramped, hutch-like wooden carriages from very early trains – you can try sitting inside one.

Making trains and controlling them

An easily missed upstairs gallery, reached from the Great Hall, houses a fascinating section on train construction and railway signals and safety.

- Old films show steam locomotives being assembled from huge parts. Great wheels are cast in one piece from molten steel poured into a sand mould.
- A display analyses famous railway accidents and the safety improvements which each generated.
- Interactive exhibits show how signal boxes track a train's position and control travel to the next stretch of line.
- Try communicating with another signal box, using bell-rings on an electric telegraph.

The Warehouse

Adjoining the Great Hall at ground level, the 'Warehouse' houses an extraordinary mixture of railways curiosities and bric à brac. Things like:

- the "Platform 9 ¾" sign from the Harry Potter films.
- a huge fleet of model trains made by an obsessive railways modeller, still busy at the age of 97.
- a working model of a visionary Edwardian electric monorail, which investors sadly failed to fund.
- the fanciest gents' urinal in the world, encased in luxuriant cast-iron foliage.

A good way to learn your way round is one of the regular Warehouse tours.

Station Hall

This huge area celebrates the beauty and luxury of old passenger carriages. It's actually on the other side of the road to the Great Hall and you can reach it by a tunnel leading from the latter.

A highlight is the royal train used by Edward VII and George V. It includes a lounge, a smoking room, a study, and a bathroom carriage. With comical frequency some carriages are studded with electric bells to summon 'Equerry' or 'Attendant', so the King need hardly move an inch to reach a button.

Stylish carriages for non-royals are present too. There's the actual carriage from which the rich old gentleman waves in the film 'The Railway Children'.

Station Hall's lighting is artistically low, which brings out the beauty of the superbly polished engines and carriages. Adjacent is a gallery of paintings about railways.

Child friendly
Many parts of the museum are made child-friendly, through things like interactive exhibits. Also, more specifically:
- A children's outdoor play area with slides and similar amusements
- Exciting travel simulator rides
- Child-oriented talks about trains

All aboard for Hogwarts School! Spot the platform sign from the Harry Potter films in the Rail Museum's 'Warehouse'

Castle Museum

In a nutshell

Housed in two 18th century former prisons, this vast museum illustrates bygone English lifestyles – mainly 18th and 19th century. Its famous centrepiece is a recreation of a large and beautiful Victorian street, where you can enter some of the shops – one of the great sights of York. Old prison cells, period furnished rooms and antique fashion clothes are amongst other features.

Contact details

Address: York Castle Museum, Eye of York, York YO1 9RY
Phone: 01904 687687
Website: **www.yorkcastlemuseum.org.uk**

Location: Map – E5.
Places nearby: **Cliffords Tower** & **Fairfax House**

Opening times and admission charges

- Open daily 9.30 am – 5 pm, apart from Christmas Day, Boxing Day and New Year's Day.
- Prices: Adults £9.09. Children (under 16 years) Free. Concessions £5 (for people aged 17 – 24 or in receipt of a means-tested welfare benefit.)
- Free entry for wheelchair users (+ 1 helper).

Note, 'YMT Card' combination ticket is available which provides entry to Castle Museum, Yorkshire Museum and Art Gallery for 12 months of repeat visits.

Planning your visit

The 'North Building' is the part which you shouldn't miss. Bring 20 pence pieces for some antique slot machines, which operate tableaux like a spiritualist séance or a prison gallows.

What it's like

'North Building': left side of Castle Museum entrance

The Period Rooms

This side starts with five rooms showing different furnishing styles from medieval through to an accurately drab 1950s room with china ducks on a dingy brown wall. There's a splendidly cluttered Victorian room with stuffed parrot under glass dome, anti-macassars on chairs and sardines laid out for teatime.

'Toy Stories'

Next there's a largish display of a wide variety of 'old toys', ranging from Victorian teddy bears to computer games from less than 20 years ago. Many visitors seem engaged by spotting things which they themselves once played with. The wide age range of the toys means that many people can thus be entertained.

'Shaping the Body'

A new exhibition which largely features fashions in clothing from 1600 to the present day – with plenty on the most recent decades. There's things like underwear through the ages and novelties like wig curlers and a caterpillar-like bellows with which 18th century gents puffed perfumed powder on their wigs. Fashionable topics, like gender identity and body image, are also seized on– as much as is possible in a museum in a former prison.

The Automaton Clock

Soon after entry to the exhibition just mentioned, on your right is the large, 18th century, gilt and jewelled 'Automaton Clock'. Every three hours this should go into action and it's a wonderful sight. Twenty jewelled stars on the clock's face rotate, while in a tableau at the front 26 little figures cross a bridge in front of a moving waterfall, simulated by rotating glass rods. At the back there's another more elaborate animated waterfall, past which more figures file. The clock used to perform these wonders at 10.06, 13.06 and 16.06 but, at the time of writing, it is awaiting repairs. On arrival at the museum ask if it is yet working.

Nostalgic kitchens

Old-fashioned kitchens of the recent past are on display and almost certainly you'll recognise a family kitchen here. But which will you see, enshrined here as a museum-piece - your granny's kitchen, your parents', or your present one?

Kirkgate Victorian Street

In this large, lovingly reconstructed street, many shops are extraordinarily beautiful – both in their elegantly ornamented shopfronts and in the artistry of the genuine Victorian goods in their windows. There are lustrous green Chinese tea caddies, coloured chemist's carboys, polished brass telescopes and magic lanterns, a finely decorated dulcimer and beautiful walking sticks made of spiral cut glass. A military tailor offers pith helmets and pistols for explorers alongside a Guardsman's bearskin and a Life Guard's helmet. In the tobacconists, don't miss the amazing pipe, made of winding lengths of china piping like a mass of spaghetti. Nor the fabulous openwork clock mechanism in the watchmaker's shop.

You can go inside several Kirkgate establishments like the toy shop, chemists, watchmakers, police station, bank and school. A couple of shops are sometimes open for business – old-fashioned sweets from one shop, old-fashioned optical toys from another.

In 2012 more space from the old prison was incorporated into back streets for Kirkgate - including some less salubrious quarters with a hint of the squalor and menace

A shop in the Victorian Street

of York's Victorian slums. Some shops have been reshaped using records of actual shops in Victorian York – like a taxidermist with a huge stuffed pike and humming birds in jewelled colours under a glass dome. Or a chemist's shop, graced with exquisite, tiny medicine phials in textured jade green glass. The greatest impact remains the sheer beauty of so many of these wonderfully crafted Victorian objects. Throughout Kirkgate they are carefully illuminated with soft lighting. On the sound effects side, bells chime, horses neigh and horse hooves clatter on cobbles. Indeed there's a coach and a hansom cab parked in the darkened street with its softly glowing shop windows. In this dreamy Victorian evening vista it would be no surprise if, from the magic lantern shop, Sherlock Holmes and Dr Watson were to amble out.

Look out for the 'Temperance Cocoa House', which contains intriguing Victorian posters for the temperance movement. One line, which the posters push, is that, if you avoid alcohol, you can get your chores done more effectively. To persuade women, getting the laundry done is the example on offer. To give temperance man-appeal, crushing a rebellion in backwoods Canada is extolled as something which a chap does better when he's sober.

Another poster, 'The Doings of Drink', manages to pack just about every imaginable alcohol-related mishap into a single crowd scene. In the midst of drunks lying on the pavement, street fights, traffic accidents, the pawning of family treasures, raids by creditors' bailiffs, and home maintenance from hell, some poor soul has gone and quietly hanged himself.

Not all of Kirkgate is the work of the museum's creators. The padded cell in the police station is a real padded cell from the old prison.

'Kirkgate' Victorian Street

'South building': right-hand side of entrance

Soon after entering this side, there are signs to a café. You may well need this if you're trying to visit the whole museum at once.

For many years the most memorable part of this section was a charming exhibition of changing fashions in clothing, plus a gallery of historic toys. But between 2014 and 2018 this is replaced by an exhibition about World War One, in line with the government's commemoration programme.

World War One Exhibition
The large exhibition touches on many varied angles on the war, though in no great depth on any of them. It's part of the 2014-18 national commemoration programme for the War's centenary years. There's a reconstructed section of a trench plus sound effects, some rifles, machine guns, pistols and gas masks. Old film on video shows tests of early tanks lumbering across wide trenches and glimpses of life on warships. In one room, where very short films are continuously repeated, there's a nice one about World War One cartoons. Some of the more unusual exhibits are rather thought-provoking:

- A horse's gas mask.

- The non-issue body armour which some shrewd soldiers bought with their own money.

- A dummy head for raising above the trench parapet to draw enemy fire.

- Lumps of moss, used for dressing wounds.

- Phoney posed photos of cheery POWs, sent by Germany to POWs' families for propaganda purposes.

Raindale Water Mill

Passing through a courtyard with outdoor games for children, you can detour to Raindale Mill, a relocated rural water-mill, which on occasion grinds corn.

The 1960s exhibition

Here are sixties record sleeves, record players, mini-skirts, a parka, a motor scooter and early Private Eye covers. You can play your choice discs on a Sixties juke box. A period film clip gives a Sixties view of the Sixties. There are thorough-sounding textboards about social changes of the period. But somehow it never really engages with the powerful emotions of the period. At the exit, peep behind the textboard on your left to see prisoners' graffiti on the former cell wall, some of it stylishly carved.

The old prison

The final part of the Museum shows cells in the old prison in which it is situated. Exhibits here do change somewhat.

At present it mainly comprises empty cells with automated projections of film clips of actors playing historic characters from the prison records. A prison life exhibition includes a Cat O' Five Tails, a branding iron and a thumbscrew, alongside pictures of the treadmill and gallows here. No way though to exhibit the woeful ventilation which sometimes actually suffocated prisoners to death.

Sometimes the exhibition has included accounts of the many political prisoners held here, like the Luddites and the Chartist campaigners for the right to vote and the Sheffield poet cum newspaper editor James Montgomery.

There's a prison visits cell where a warder sat in a barred space between prisoner and visitor and a spacious cell where highwayman Dick Turpin spent his last night before execution.

Jorvik Viking Centre

In a nutshell

Tenth century York was a major Viking town. This museum uses engaging, child-friendly methods, like a ride in fun-fair cars round reconstructed Viking streets, to show everyday life there. Since the Vikings weren't strong on writing history books, all evidence comes from Viking rubbish dug up on this very spot when the Coppergate shopping centre was built in the 1970s. The museum shows how rubbish and residues were studied for this purpose. In April 2017 the Jorvik Centre re-opened after a long closure following December 2015 flood damage. If you've visited before, you'll notice some new twists to the 'fun fair ride' described next.

Contact details

Address: Jorvik Viking Centre, Coppergate, York YO1 9WT
Phone: 01904 615 505
Website: **www.jorvik-viking-centre.co.uk**

Location: Map – bottom left of E4.
Places nearby: **Merchant Adventurers Hall** & **Fairfax House**.

Opening Times and Admission prices

- Open every day except Christmas Eve to Boxing Day. 10 am – 5 pm
- Prices: Adult £11. Concession £9. Child (5-15 years) £8. Family tickets from £32.
- One entry ticket gives unlimited visits for 12 months.
- Tickets available for combinations of Jorvik, DIG, Barley Hall & the Micklegate Bar Museum.
- Book tickets on-line to avoid the queues here at some times of year.

What it's like

The museum's starting point is a hall with a glass floor over recreation of the 1970s archaeological excavations which revealed Viking lifestyles of 10th century York. Beneath your feet are trenches, drains, bits of ancient wood and stone and the odd amber treasure. On audios, the original archaeologists describe the experience and photos are projected on the walls.

Next comes Jorvik's highlight – the 16 minute time travel round Viking streets. You climb into a little car on a rail, which takes you round reconstructed Viking streets rather like a ghost train. There are three seats to each car. A commentary comes through mini-speakers in the language of your choice. There are 14 languages to choose from - Chinese, Japanese and Arabic included. English speakers get a choice of 'Adult' or 'Child' commentary. For this adult anyway, the child-level commentary proved just the ticket – very informative but not a distraction from the sights.

Your car winds slowly round very muddy streets lined with life-size thatched, wooden Viking houses and yards, divided by wicker fences. As you pass them, animated figures in Viking dress wave goods, which they are making or selling, and make comments in the Scandinavian dialect of the time. Now, as in pre-flood Jorvik, these figures are artificially animated mannequins but the quality of the animation has improved so that some are very, very convincing. A family challenge: among some 30 animated artificial figures are one or two real humans in Viking dress – can you spot them?

And it's not just Vikings who are skillfully animated. There are moving dogs, cats, squeaking little pigs and a wicked rat who licks scraps from a butcher's chopping block. Most realistic of all are some recently caught eels, writhing in their death-throes.

One Viking chap is busy hollowing out a wooden cup with a pole-lathe woodturning machine. 'Coppergate', this area's historic name, comes from Viking for 'street of the cup makers'. Another fellow makes combs from antlers, for York's Vikings seemed a coiffure-minded lot, since many antler combs were found here.

Rough and ready smells pervade this Viking York. And not least around one of pre-flood Jorvik's best known characters. This is a fellow on an open air toilet, wad of moss in hand, Viking hygiene for the use of.

Plenty new characters have appeared since the flood, all based on archaeological evidence. There's a Christian priest, Irish slaves and an Asian trader, for instance, and an enrapt spieler of Norse sagas. No need to understand the latter's Viking lingo, for the gist of his tale is projected beside him.

The display cases
After the ride come display cases showing actual Viking brooches, combs, board games, tools and other implements, plus information about Viking life and how the latter was deduced from scientific study of Viking rubbish.

What might interest children in this sort of scientific archaeology? On display is a massive Viking turd from old Jorvik, eight ounces of it - genuine, totally recognisable and sitting in a glass case, bold as brass. Details are given how microscopic analysis uncovered the owner's diet and the nasty intestinal worms which afflicted Jorvik folk. If keen not to miss this wonder, it's in the fifth cabinet on your left after leaving the ride.

The display cases mix things discovered under the Jorvik Centre with more spectacular Viking items from elsewhere

– huge spearheads, swords, jewellery, coins and locks. An attendant in a Viking outfit will hammer you out a Viking coin. There are two complete skeletons of Viking women found in York.

One notable display shows Viking panpipes and bone flutes, which were found on this very spot, while a touchscreen video panel plays you tuneful tones from various Viking musical instruments.

Jorvik's shop
You exit via Jorvik's shop where you can buy a Viking board game, 'King's Table'. Or gear up for battle with pricey battle axes and swords. Or for a banquet with £8 bottles of mead and vast drinking horns which make you down that mead in one.

Interested in the sort of scientific archaeology pioneered at Jorvik? Nearby in St Saviourgate is Jorvik's sister enterprise, DIG, where there's a clever, child-oriented, hour-long simulation of taking part in an archaeological dig.

DIG - a child-friendly chance to play at archaeology

In a nutshell
A clever, interesting and informative simulation of digging as an archaeologist. It's indoors, clean and dry – and historic finds are guaranteed!

Contact details
Address: DIG, St Saviour's Church, St Saviourgate, York YO1 8NN
Phone: 01904 615 505
Website: **www.digyork.com/**

Location: Map - bottom left of F3.

Places nearby **Merchant Adventurers Hall** & **Jorvik** are moderately near.

Opening times and admission prices
- Open every day except Christmas Eve to Boxing Day: 10 am – 5 pm, (last admission 4 pm.)
- Prices: Adult £6.50. Child £6. Concession £6. Family tickets start at £20.
- One entry ticket gives unlimited visits for 12 months.
- Tickets available for combinations of DIG, Jorvik, Barley Hall & the Micklegate Bar Museum.

Book tickets on-line to avoid waiting for space on the accompanied tours.

What it's like
In this converted church, parties of five or six people are led by an archaeologist on a simulated archaeological dig. You dig in indoor bays filled with very fine rubber fragments which simulate soil but without the dirt or wet. You get a plastic trowel and then choose from four bays: Victorian, medieval, Viking, and Roman. Hidden in each bay are objects from the period. In the Roman bay, for instance, we found pottery fragments and stone missiles from a ballista siege weapon. In the Viking bay, some slag from iron smelting got turned up. Children proved especially deft at this, ferreting out Roman coins which the adults had missed.

Next, your archaeologist shares with you some boxes of actual bones and other objects found in Viking rubbish dumps in York. You go through the ways in which the bones of different animals are identified and the clues about the animal's age at death and how they were butchered and what might be deduced from this. This is the sort of scientific detective work through which the secrets of Viking Jorvik were uncovered.

Unless you book in advance, you may sometimes need to wait a bit to do your dig with the archaeologist. While you wait, there are exhibits to look at about modern scientific archaeology.

Sometimes there are also outdoor tours of real archaeological digs taking place nearby.

Museum Gardens, Abbey Ruins and Observatory

No-one should leave York without visiting these lovely, free access gardens at its heart (B&C3 on the map). They contain the largest surviving section of the Roman fortress, which became incorporated into the medieval City Walls (see end of Chapter 3). Near this most impressive piece of Roman fortress, on the Museum side of the wall, is a charming, shady fern garden where the stones are a mix of medieval fragments and fossils.

Museum Gardens also contains the picturesque ruins of St Mary's Abbey, destroyed after seizure by Henry VIII. In its heyday, the Abbey was famed for the luxury and laxity of its monks' lifestyle. When in 1130 some serious-minded monks called for something a bit more monk-like, they were practically lynched as spoilsports before fleeing, under the Archbishop's protection, to found Fountains Abbey. You can read verbatim the appalled Archbishop's report on the scandal:
http://cistercians.shef.ac.uk/fountains/history/app4.php .

In the 1820s, the Abbey ruins were incorporated into a sort of science zone created privately by the Yorkshire Philosophical Society, a band of citizen enthusiasts for science. The gardens were their botanical garden, containing every native British tree. They built the Yorkshire Museum to house their fossil collection and in 1833 the astronomical observatory. Upstairs in the Yorkshire Museum is a room which commemorates them. The Yorkshire Philosophical Society still flourishes.

A recent addition to the area beyond the Abbey ruins is a garden for exotic types of edible plant. At some stage this will lead on into a new sculpture garden.

Just before you enter the edible plants garden, look on the ground on your left for a new mosaic about northern England's geology. It's embedded with colourful polished pebbles and the odd fossil. It commemorates pioneering geologists, 200 years ago, in the vogue for scientific study which led to the creation of the Museum and its Gardens.

In summer sometimes there are displays of hawks and owls in Museum Gardens. For much of the year, there are plenty of bold squirrels and pigeons for children to feed.

Observatory in Museum Gardens
Look on the Yorkshire Museum's website or ask at its counter about the varying opening times of the Observatory. During daytime openings you can see its large 1850 telescope. As the earth rotates, this telescope is rotated in the opposite direction by a motor worked by a pendulum weight, so you can keep a particular star in view. Sometimes there are night-time openings when you can view moon, planets or stars through this telescope.

The Yorkshire Museum

In a nutshell
Particularly memorable exhibits are objects which convey the human side of Roman York, plus some well-preserved Anglo-Saxon swords and helmet. Children may specially enjoy a chance to feed by hand Alan, a Virtual Reality dinosaur in an exhibition on Jurassic era Yorkshire.

Address: Museum Gardens, York YO1 7FR
Phone: 01904 687687
Website: **www.yorkshiremuseum.org.uk**

Location: Map – C3. In Museum Gardens
Places nearby: **Visit York**, **Kings Manor**, **Art Gallery**.

Opening times and prices
- Open everyday except for 25 and 26 December, and 1 January. Open 10am - 5pm
- Adult £6.81. Child (under 16) Free.
- Concessions £4 (for people aged 17 – 24 or in receipt of a means-tested welfare benefit.)
- 'YMT Card' combination ticket available which provides entry to Yorkshire Museum, Castle Museum and Art Gallery for 12 months of visits

What it's like:

Roman York
A key exhibition displays Roman objects from York, once a major Roman army town. There are lamps, bracelets, needles, fancy cloak clasps, a board game. There's even a large coil of a Roman era woman's hair complete with jet hairpins, all perfectly preserved within a sealed lead coffin. One exhibit reconstructs the likely faces of some Roman

Family scene on Roman tomb, Yorkshire Museum

York citizens from their skulls. They seem to have come from every corner of the Roman Empire.

The human touch comes over most from the Roman tombstones. Some are carved with scenes of family life or touching inscriptions of grief. Look out for Julia Velva's tomb where the family tableau includes her daughter's pet bird.

On a table map of modern York, you can lift little doors to see which Roman objects have been found where. There are some very basic children's activities with building bricks and coin impressions, for this Museum is keen to engage children.

Other displays, inc. 'Feeding Alan'
The museum's treasures periodically move on and off display. There's often an exhibition about medieval York in

the basement and a fossil-oriented exhibition on the ground floor.

Most recently the latter is a display of local dinosaur remains and other fossils from the Jurassic era. For adults, star of the show will probably be a huge, fossilized sea dinosaur, a plesiosaur. For children, it will definitely be 'Feeding Alan', a chance to feed by hand a large dinosaur, thanks to Virtual Reality technology. Alan was a local dinosaur, whose chunky vertebrae are on display and who now makes a come-back on a large digital screen. Children take turns to don Virtual Reality headgear and, advised by an instructor, can make a berry-laden branch wave around under Alan's nose on the large digital screen. Whereupon Alan leans over and snaps it up in full view of everyone.

Some notable items which may be on display (ask museum staff for their whereabouts):

- The Anglo-Saxon helmet found while York's Coppergate shopping centre was being built.

- The Anglo-Saxon 'Gilling sword' found by a nine year boy.

- A Yorkshire Viking hoard of silver coins – spot the coin with the Arabic inscription, all the way from Samarkand.

- The lovely medieval gold and sapphire 'Middleham Jewel' pendant.

- The Star Carr headdresses – from 9000 BC, these are deer antlers on severed skull tops, once worn by humans in Yorkshire for unexplained purposes.

York Art Gallery

In a nutshell
Large and lively mixture of modern ceramics and historic English and Continental paintings. Often some activities for children.
NB Until 25 November 2018, the exhibition: 'Strata, Rock, Dust, Stars'. There's a room of screens of film from ice caves in Iceland. Another screen showing an arty conception of a star's life cycle. And a room with a triple screen showing a lengthy medley of erupting volcanoes, crystalline sulphur and enigmatic scientific activity and apparatus.

Contact details
Address: York Art Gallery, Exhibition Square, York YO1 7EW
Phone: (01904) 687687
Website: **www.yorkartgallery.org.uk**

Location: Map – C2.
Places nearby :Opposite **Bootham Bar** gate in city Walls and next to **Kings Manor**

Opening times
- Open every day.
- Monday – Friday: 10 am – 5 pm
- Saturday: 10 am – 6 pm
- Sunday: 11 am – 4 pm

Prices
- Adult (aged over 25): £6.82
- Accompanied children (under 17 years): free.
- 17 – 24 year olds: £4
- People on income related benefits: £4
- Cheaper entry via York Museums Trust Card (**www.yorkmuseumstrust.org.uk**)
- Special rates for York residents.

Café
On right hand side, if facing the building – indoor seating plus outdoor tables near the fountains. There are snacks and, earlier in the day, meals.

What it's like
The 2015 relaunch has brought a fresh, visitor-friendly touch to this Gallery and many extra art works on display.

Upstairs is a major new ceramics section. There are some celebrity items – like 'Melanie', Grayson Perry's ceramic tribute to beauty of larger women, as seen on TV. There's an expanse of immensely varied, richly textured pots, plates and sculptures in every possible shade of brown and yellow. Here and there are some most inventive and entertaining ceramics. Search for Ian Godfrey's fantasy animals and sparkling pools of turquoise glass.

It's not possible to reliably describe the exhibits on the ground floor because repeatedly this is cleared to house large exhibitions for six months at a time. But, when space is available, items like the following make an appearance.

There's a set of paintings of York, past and present, which are often surprising. They include a memorable Lowry. Invited to paint York, Lowry picked a strange, long distance view of York Minster, which you'll never see on a postcard. In the foreground are railtracks, smoky factory chimneys, cooling tower and brick tenement housing – with the Minster itself a distant smudge behind smog. You can take Lowry away from grimy Salford but you can't take grimy Salford away from Lowry!

There's a collection of intriguing Victorian paintings which seem to capture stories. They freeze-frame human scenes and the viewer can study clues to work out what's going on.

Sometimes there are materials for trying your own artwork in a particular genre. One regular feature is a table where you can craft a sombre 'vanitas' or 'memento mori' piece to echo gloomy 16th century musings on life's transience, on display nearby.

Ask at the entry desk for 'Portrait Interactive'. On this, you line up your reflection on an ingenious screen on which a sequence of the gallery's portraits appear. Then a photo is taken. Next the historic portrait re-appears with your own face reincarnated in the head-dress or background of the painting. The new you lasts but a minute or so, but it's time enough for people to snap their portrait with their phones.

York's Chocolate Story

In a nutshell
Partly guided tour, partly on your own, a digital-age time trip to York's famous chocolate industry, the world of Rowntrees and Terrys of York. You'll taste chocolate like a connoisseur, see how chocolate is made, and maybe design a chocolate bar wrapper of your own.

Contact details
Address: Chocolate, King's Square, York YO1 7LD
Phone: 0845-4989411
Website: yorkschocolatestory.com

Location: Map – E3.
Places nearby: entrance to the Shambles, Minster end.

Opening times and prices
- Open daily 10 am – 6 pm, except Christmas Day & New Year's Day.
- Adults £11.50. Seniors & Students £10.50. Children (5 -16 years) £9.50. Under 5s free. Family £39.95
- Online booking: c. 10% reduction.

What it's like

The experience starts in the chocolate café while you're waiting for a tour (ten minutes perhaps). Chocolate goodies are on offer – all sorts of speciality chocolate. Special pots for making hot chocolate are also on sale - though not the fabled chocolate teapot of Yorkshire repartee. There's plenty hot chocolate to drink, either plain or flavoured with orange, mint or chilli. This chocolate shop cum café can be visited independent of the tour of 'Chocolate'.

Your tour takes place in groups of around 10 people. First step is a test-bite of chocolate and a briefing on how the chocolate trade itself would assess its taste. You're shown a 'chocolate wheel' with a 60 plus list of categories for rating what you've just tasted. ('Pine', 'heather' and 'orange' we might just have expected. But who gets the chocolate which has scored well on 'leather' or 'rubber'?)

Next it's astral time-travel back to chocolate's origins in ancient Mexico. Dramatic film effects take you through a splendidly starry sky to chocolate-minded Aztec gods and a powerful panorama of serious goings-on at an Aztec temple. An original Aztec-style drink of unsweetened cold chocolate is passed round for us to taste. 'Disgusting', shouts a little girl, helpfully adding a classification for that chocolate wheel. The drink does indeed convey how those Aztecs needed help from Messrs Rowntrees and Terry to bring out the best from their cocoa beans. Too much fussing around at that fancy temple, one suspects, and not enough time on the chocolate wheel.

Then there's more dramatic film of the Spanish conquest of Mexico, when the Aztecs' chocolate joined gold and silver in the loot bound for Europe. Visual effects at 'Chocolate' are brilliantly done. The next room seems at first to be hung with framed portraits of the Rowntree and Terry dynasties, who founded Britain's chocolate industry in the 18th and

19th centuries. Then the people in the pictures come to life and start telling you their stories and arguing with the character in the frame next to them. Whilst they argue, we eat more chocolate.

Further on there's a 'virtual chocolate factory', where you can make some, well, virtual chocolate. The actual process is too lengthy to replicate, so this is a simulation on illuminated panels. Brave youngsters from your party rev steel wheels to crush cocoa bean icons to the right consistency, whereupon a simulated splodge of chocolate appears on the next panel. More ingredients get mixed in via touch-pads and a final virtual chocolate product appears on screen. Whilst you watch, you can munch non-virtual, raw, crushed cocoa beans – and very nice too.

Next demonstration is the creation of hand-made chocolates – from cooling at the speed which forms the tastiest chocolate crystals to the filling of moulds. An angled mirror means that folk of all heights can follow the plot. And everyone tastes the result.

After this, in your own time you look round exhibits about the 'Capital of Chocolate', whence flowed out Aeros, Smarties, Black Magic, Terry's Chocolate Orange, and the best seller of all time, Kit Kat. You can learn how Kit Kat's appearance has changed over the decades and about its 42 different flavours in Japan. There's a machine where you can design your own chocolate bar wrapper and e-mail it back home – or enter it for a chocolate wrapper competition.

You can watch early TV commercials for York chocolate brands. Or play the archive film of your choice from videos about the Quaker Rowntrees, who strove for a sense of a caring community among their workers. There's footage of the firm's marvellous convalescent centre in 1940s Scarborough where everyone is singing and playing with such gusto that it boggles your mind how there could be anything wrong with them.

Look out for Mr York. He's a large, saucy-looking automaton who by the 1930s had made himself a true national icon, promoting Rowntrees chocolate with his alarmingly mobile eyebrows. Below him is an entertaining video about his career.

Look out, too, for a machine which quizzes you on your tastes, then chooses a chocolate bar to suit you. When you exit to the shop, you'll find it on sale.

How long might you spend at 'Chocolate' altogether? Perhaps between 60 and 90 minutes. Do children enjoy it? From watching our tour party, that's a definite 'Yes'.

York St Mary's Arts Centre

Contact details

Address: York St Mary's, Castlegate, York YO1 9RN

Website: **www.yorkstmarys.org.uk**

Location: top left of map square E5.

Places nearby: Fairfax House, Jorvik, Cliffords Tower and Castle Museum.

Opening times: Wednesday to Sunday, 11 – 4. *Free entry*.

This beautiful medieval church is now re-used for a series of changing art exhibitions. Often the latter are large modern art installations. For instance, one involved hanging a thousand small glass bells round the church. Another created a long indoor pool along which lighted candles floated. For the current exhibition, see the website.

The church building itself is also worth seeing.

The Stained Glass Centre

Contact details
Address: St Martin-cum-Gregory, Micklegate, York YO1 6LN
Phone: 01904-611687
Website: **www.stainedglasscentre.org**

Location: Map – C5. Next St Martin's Lane.
Places nearby: All Saints Church, North Street. Micklegate Bar.

This new museum is gradually evolving. Located in a disused medieval church, at present it provides:

- Periodic interesting guided tours round this church's stained glass plus displays about how stained glass was made and painted.
- Periodic talks and practical courses and workshops about making stained glass.

If interested, monitor their website for the above events or for expansion of the Centre's programme.

MUSEUMS JUST OUTSIDE EAST YORK

Yorkshire Museum of Farming / Danelaw Centre for Living History

In a nutshell
An impressively large, child-oriented Viking village and a Roman fort now overshadow the farming museum side. These may interest families seeking somewhere outdoors where children can explore. It's so large that you can easily spend an afternoon here. Phone first to check that these parts of the museum are accessible, for on weekdays in term time they're reserved for school parties. On the farm museum side, there are sheep, hens and ponies to feed or

pet. On Sundays, Easter – September, there are half-mile steam train rides from next to the museum.

Contact details
Address: Yorkshire Museum of Farming, Murton Park, York, YO19 5UF
Phone: (01904) 489966
Website: **www.murtonpark.co.uk**

How to get there
Three miles east from centre of York, it's just off the A166 near the junction with the A64.
From central York, a 10 minute bus ride plus 15 minute walk on the No. 10 bus towards Stamford Bridge. See YorkshireTravel.Net for timetable and walking instructions. Board the bus either outside York Rail Station or in Merchantgate, near Merchant Adventurers' Hall. Bus services X46, X4 & 746 also ply this route, sometimes 5 buses per hour. Ask for a stop near Grimston Court. The Grimston Bar Park & Ride stop is also close to the Museum.

Opening times and prices (not yet confirmed for 2018)
- Usually the museum is open daily, April till autumn, 10 am – 5 pm, plus some weekends at other times. Phone to check.
- Adults £7. Concessions £6. Children £5 (under 3s are free). Family Ticket £20.

Yorkshire Air Museum, Elvington, near York

In a nutshell
The Air Museum is on a carefully preserved World War Two airbase - huts and hangars exactly as they were. Some exhibits, like photos and campaign stories, are primarily of interest to people who knew the airmen commemorated.

Among exhibits of wider interest:

- Some 50 vintage aircraft, including the Spitfire, Hurricane, Mosquito and Messerschmitt, and many later jet warplanes like Meteor, Lightning, Canberra, and a huge Victor bomber.
- Much World War Two memorabilia – living quarters, posters, equipment.
- A display about life in the gun turrets of World War Two bombers.
- A recreation of the Officers' Mess for the Free French airmen based here.
- Some World War 2 planes are still flown periodically. There's an old NAAFI-style restaurant. Museum staff and many visitors radiate RAF knowledge and connections.

Contact details
Address: Yorkshire Air Museum, Elvington, York YO41 4AU
Phone: (01904) 608595
Website: **www.yorkshireairmuseum.org**

Opening times, prices and facilities
- Open daily, except Christmas Day & Boxing Day. Summer 10 am – 5 pm; Winter 10 am – 4 pm.
- Adults £10. Seniors, Servicemen & Students £8. Children (5-15 years) £5. Families £26.

How to get there
It's situated off B1228 - before Elvington, 6 miles south-east from York's centre.

Check with Museum website for current bus times. At time of writing:

- Monday – Saturday, No. 36 bus from Merchantgate, central York at: 11.15 am & 13.15 pm. 25 minute bus journey.
- Buses back leave Museum 2.34 pm & 4.34 pm.
- On Sundays, 18A bus departs from York War Memorial, Station Rise at 10 am & 12 pm.
- Sunday buses back leave Air Museum 1.40 pm & 3.40 pm.
- NB Sunday buses stop in Elvington Lane, not right outside the Air Museum.

Ruins of St Mary's Abbey, Museum Gardens

CHAPTER FIVE
ADDITIONAL INFORMATION

Calendar of Annual York Festivals

York Residents Festival
In 2018, January 27 - 28
York residents get a weekend of free or low cost access to tourist attractions in York and nearby. For non-residents this means:
- Some buildings may be open which normally aren't, like 'behind the scenes' at the Opera House.
- The mainstream attractions may be more crowded.

You need a resident's York Card for free entry. A programme is available from **Visit York**.

Jorvik Viking Festival
In 2018, February 12 – 18
A week-long festival at schools half-term in February, climaxing at a weekend. Typical events include mock battles, plays and story readings about Vikings, children dressing up as Vikings, a Best Beard competition, and academic talks about the Viking world. On many days there are markets run by Norwegian, Swedish and Polish enthusiasts for Viking culture, who wear Viking clothes and sell high quality Viking-revival jewellery, helmets, battleaxes, furs, horn combs and cloth made Viking-style. They also demonstrate Viking craft techniques. Also, some try-for-yourself Viking combat for children. The Festival often ends with a spectacular event – like a Viking-style boat burning. Admission charges for some events but not others. Full programme: **www.jorvikvikingfestival.co.uk**

York Chocolate Festival.
In 2018, March 29 - April 2
An Easter festival, celebrating York's history as a major chocolate manufacturer, the city of Rowntrees, Terrys etc. In Parliament Street, central York, there's a chocolate market and demonstrations of local craftsmanship in

Scenes from York Festivals

Mock battle in Museum Gardens during February's Viking Festival

September's Festival of Traditional Dance

chocolate making - and a chance to try your own hand at the latter. There's plenty for children. Sometimes chocolate-related activities also occur at other York attractions. For programme: **www.yorkchocolatefestival.co.uk**

York Open Studios
In 2018, April 14 – 15 & April 21 – 22
Probably more of interest to local residents than to visitors on holiday, during two weekends each spring nearly 100 York artists and craft workers display and sell their creations – usually in their own homes. Paintings, pottery, wall fabrics, stained glass window decorations, jewellery, exotic domed birdhouses, zany two-spouted teapots…the variety is entrancing. A nice feature is the mix of professional artists and talented hobbyists. You get a printed brochure with a map for finding each artist's exhibition. For all details: **www.yorkopenstudios.co.uk/**

Eboracum Roman Festival
In 2018, 1 – 3 June
After 2017's excellent event, the revived Roman Festival seems set to become a highlight of York's Festival Year. Timed for the last weekend of schools' summer half-term week, the Festival combines scholarly information with eye-catching spectacles which appeal to adults and children alike. On show in Museum Gardens were Roman soldiers demonstrating battlefield tactics with sword, spear and interlocking shields, while the secrets of a legionary's kit bag went on full display. Costumed re-enactors presented Roman surgical equipment (surprisingly advanced), guided you in playing Roman board games, or explained working replicas of Roman bows, slings and light siege weapons. There were legionary parades, guided walks round York Roman sites, and talks about local archaeological investigations. Children got their own series of history talks. They also got a chance to dress up en masse in Roman armour, receive Roman drill practice, then fight

a barbarian army composed of ... their parents. The latter, lacking Roman drill, got soundly walloped – there's barbarians for you!

For details, see the Yorkshire Museum's website: **www.yorkmuseumstrust.org.uk/eboracum-roman-festival/**

Charge of the children's legion, Roman Festival 2017

York Folk Music Weekend
In 2018, June 1 - 3
Often first weekend in June, a weekend of free folk music around the **Black Swan** pub, Peaseholme Green, York. Programme from **www.blackswanfolkclub.org.uk/**

York Festival of Ideas
In 2018, June 5 – 17
Probably more of interest to local residents than to visitors on holiday, this vast, unusual festival can be understood only by looking at its website, such is the number, variety and originality of the presentations on offer. During a fortnight each June some 120 plus lectures, discussions or displays take place free of charge, hosted by York University. Some are within York's old walled city but most are on the attractive campus of York University, within

walking distance from the former. Anyone can attend any session but usually you need to book in advance. For all details: **yorkfestivalofideas.com/**

'Shakespeare's Rose Theatre'
In 2018, June 25 – September 2
A totally new event: in a temporary simulation of an Elizabethan theatre next to Cliffords Tower, four Shakespeare plays will be performed with Elizabethan stagecraft and ambience. The plays are: 'Macbeth', 'Romeo and Juliet', 'A Midsummer's Night's Dream' and 'Richard III'. For details: **www.shakespearesrosetheatre.com**

Great Yorkshire Fringe, York
In 2018, July 19 – 29
York's newest major festival, heading fast to become top event of the York festival year. Three cleverly decorated marquees, close together in central York's Parliament Street, host jazz musicians, dancers, magicians and, most of all, stand-up comedians - both established comics and total novices. There's good variety in a fast changing programme. Some events suit children – like 2016's 'Amazing Bubble Show' where children could stand inside a giant bubble amidst spinning bubbles, smoke-filled bubbles and bubbling bubbles. Amidst the marquees are plentiful hot food stalls and makeshift bars. Tickets can be bought on-line or on the spot. For programme and booking: **www.greatyorkshirefringe.com**

York Minster stone carvers' festival
In 2018, August 17 - 19
On August 17, an Open Day at the Minster Stoneyard, a workshop next to York Minster which replaces weatherworn stone carvings from the Minster. You can watch the skilled craftsmen at work. Ask at the Minster for directions. It's followed on August 18 & 19 by a craftsmen's stone carving competition in Dean's Park, next to York

Minster. At 3.30 pm on August 19, their carvings are auctioned publicly.

Micklegate Soapbox Challenge
In 2018, August 27
A family fun event for August Bank Holiday Monday. Fifty homemade four-wheel or three-wheel carts race down historic Micklegate from near Micklegate Bar. Each vehicle is in turn hauled up a steep ramp, then released with its driver to roll down Micklegate, while its journey is timed – usually 30 – 60 seconds. Vehicles are crafted as things like a giant beer can, a coffin, a dragon, a bull, a bath and so on. Some release coloured smoke or bubbles - or squirt water on the crowd. Expect a 10 am starting time and a complete set of races by mid-day. Then a second set in the afternoon. Ample street food and drink is nearby and there's a cheery, if crowded, atmosphere. Expect a children's funfair on Ouse Bridge at the end of Micklegate.

York Festival of Traditional Dance
In 2018, September 8 – 9
Often the first complete weekend in September. Displays of different types of Morris dancing, sword dancing etc – usually in Parliament Street and Kings Square. Details from **www.ebormorris.org.uk**

York Mystery Plays
In 2018, September 9 & 16
Detailed description and weblink are supplied after the Festival Calendar. Performed on these two consecutive Sundays, this will be the version staged on wagons in multiple locations.

Festival of Food and Drink
In 2018, September 21 – 30
Each September, much to try and buy – chiefly in Parliament Street. See: **www.yorkfoodfestival.com**

York Mediale
In 2018, September 27 – October 6
This major new biennial festival advertises "a 10-day citywide celebration of exhibitions, installations, performances, workshops" by leading digital artists from around the world. One element will probably be lightshows and light installations around historic buildings, as in the former 'Illuminating York' festival which it supersedes. Other aspects are yet to be revealed – see **yorkmediale.com**

Aesthetica Festival of Short Films
In 2018, November 7 – 11
Remarkable regular festival of c. 300 international short films (10 – 30 minutes), shown in myriad venues all round central York. Films range from 3 to 30 minutes in length and are programmed by genres like 'Animation', 'Comedy', 'Thriller', 'Documentary' etc. Each venue shows sets of five or six films from a particular genre and you can buy a reasonably priced universal pass and flit from venue to venue. Without Herculean effort, it is possible to see 100 of the films in the course of four days. See **www.asff.co.uk** .

St Nicholas Fayre
In 2018, November 15 – December 23
A bustling Christmas Market in Parliament Street in the centre of York – sometimes crowded at weekends. It usually starts mid /late November and runs for four weeks until Christmas.

Christmas Ice Trail
In 2018, now rescheduled for February 2 in 2019
Normally this has been on the weekend closest to mid-December. Various ice sculptures are displayed in old streets around Stonegate, 11 am – 5 pm, along with Christmas food and drink stalls (previously known as 'Festival of Angels'). In recent years, delays in announcing the date have become routine. And now it's been timetabled

for actually after Christmas! For background on the ice sculptures:
www.glacialart.com/glacial-art-on-the-york-ice-trail

Christmas season in York

During the first half of December in particular, York has a strong Christmas atmosphere, especially around Stonegate, the Minster, and Petergate. Often there's a Christmas market in Parliament Street throughout this period. Many British people visit York to get themselves into a Christmas mood. In some years many shops in Stonegate and Petergate have beautiful Christmas window displays.

Stonegate at Christmas

For the epicentre of Stonegate's Christmas atmosphere, try the new (2016) German Christmas shop, Kathe Wohlfart, at 19 Stonegate (formerly the Mulberry Hall shop). A splendid 15th century building hosts more high quality Christmas decorations than you'll find under one roof anywhere else in Britain. There are whole rooms of 'Christmas Pyramids', those traditional German whirligig devices, where heat rising from candles makes Wise Men and Shepherds rotate forever around that Crib. Christmas tree decorations come in carved wood and crystal, as well as shiny baubles, and the Advent Calendars are true works of art. Besides the most distinctively German items are interesting panels explaining their traditional origins. If this shop continues as a year-round Christmas shop, it is fast heading for recognition as one of the Sights of York.

Christmas events at York Minster
Visit **http://yorkminster.org/whats-on.html** for carol services and other Christmas music events.

The most popular is the 'Nine Lessons and Carols' service held on Christmas Eve. But it's so popular, and thus so hard to get into, that a duplicate service is sometimes scheduled days earlier.

Among other events on the Minster website, an increasingly popular, beautiful Christmas service is the Swedish 'Sankta Lucia' Advent celebration. It's usually held early on a Friday evening during the fortnight before Christmas. Choirs come from Sweden to perform this ceremony, which has Viking era origins and is hosted thanks to York's Viking connections. It starts with a procession through the darkened cathedral of singing, white robed Swedish choir girls, carrying lighted candles, led by a girl with a crown of seven lighted candles who represents St Lucia. Beside them are 'Star Boy' choristers in star-studded pointed hats, who represent the Three Wise Men, Swedish style. For photos, try 'Lucia, York Minster' on Google Images.

Christmas pantomime at York's Theatre Royal
Overseas visitors, you haven't truly sampled British culture without a traditional Christmas pantomime – and every year in York there's a panto starring our most famous

'pantomime dame', Berwick Kaler. Don't worry that panto is supposed to be for children: Berwick Kaler's audience can be over 90% adult, many of whom have been coming to his shows every year since childhood. Berwick Kaler directs the show too and with a heavy slant to raucous comedy and improvisation. Rarely does he let the storyline interfere with a chance for a good joke. The panto season may run from early December to late January. For details see: **www.yorktheatreroyal.co.uk**

York Mystery Plays

Every four years many of these astonishing, colourful, medieval, short religious plays are performed by ordinary York citizens outdoors, free of charge, on two consecutive Sunday afternoons in summer. The next time will be September 2018. See **www.yorkmysteryplays.co.uk**. (Much less regularly, special professional performances have been staged in York Minster and Museum Gardens, for which payment is required.)

What the Plays are like

First recorded in 1377, the 'Mystery Plays' derive from medieval York, where each commercial Guild presented an open-air play about a different Bible story during an annual religious festival. The plays were moved round York in a procession of wagons - resembling the processions which continue today at religious fiestas in Spain and Italy. In today's four yearly community productions, as in medieval times, the plays are performed by local people, some from surviving York Guilds. Now, as then, wooden wagons are used as stages and are pushed by hand to different locations in York's Old Town and repeat performances are given open air for free.

Around 12 different plays are performed during the afternoon, each by a different team of York citizens. Typical

Mystery Play on cart outside St William's College

places are Museum Gardens, Deans Garden, the Green opposite St William's College and St Sampsons Square. Each team of actors in turn pushes their wagon to each location and performs their short play there. You can choose one location and in due course each play will come to you. See the website for the large differences between start and finish times at different locations depending on the order in which wagons visit them. Start time at the first location may be 11 a.m. whereas finish time at the last may be 5.30 pm.

The original medieval scripts are used, which are in powerful, poetic Old English. Special effects are medieval and low tech. For the Ascension, for instance, a white cloud of cloth gets lowered down over Jesus, who rises up behind it on a trapeze seat. The Jaws of Hell literally open under the stage and long dead souls coming marching out, led by Adam and Eve, apple in hand.

The plays reach into the audience too. The whale in the Creation play sometimes squirts the audience from its blowhole and Adam has spat that apple into the front rows. Recently the front rows were issued with cabbage leaves to pelt the procession to Calvary. At the Last Judgement, devils may stride into the audience, sometimes on stilts.

You can come and go as you please. If intending to watch all the plays, bring refreshments. If you are not, don't miss the Last Judgement, which is particularly powerful.

'Visit York' tourist information service

'Visit York' is York's official tourist information service. Particularly noteworthy is its on-line, computerised service for choosing and booking hotels, hostels etc. Its office is near York Minster on the main road from the Rail Station, almost opposite Museum Gardens.

Contact details
Address: 'Visit York', 1 Museum Street, York, YO1 7DT
Phone: +44 (0) 1904 550099
Email: **info@visityork.org**
Website: **www.visityork.org/**
Location: Map – border of C3 & D3.
Places nearby: Assembly Rooms, Yorkshire Museum, Barley Hall.
Opening hours
Monday – Saturday 9 am – 5 pm. Sunday 10 am – 4 pm.

Visit York's two guidebooks
Both guidebooks include much on York attractions, plus maps with the same reference grid as in this book. The 'Full Visitor Guide' also has detailed, informative listings of hotels and other types of accommodation. You can either download it from Visit York's website or collect it from Visit York's office. The 'Mini-Guide' can be picked up at

Visit York's office and often elsewhere in the City, like Park & Ride sites, hotels and museums.

Types of information provided by Visit York
Visit York's office, website and guidebooks include information on the following:
- Organised tours of York or Yorkshire, including customised tours
- Ghost Walks and Boat Trips
- Theatres and concerts
- Smart places to shop, four Shopping Trails even!

The Visit York office also supplies some excellent special topic leaflets, like one on York's churches and an accommodation-booking service as follows.

Finding hotels & other accommodation

'Visit York' accommodation-finding service
Much the most useful resource is **Visit York**'s on-line accommodation-finding service. This covers a great variety – from luxury hotels to budget guesthouses and hostels, self-catering and camping – and you can book on-line without booking fees.

It can be accessed via **www.visityork.org/** - look for the 'Book your stay' section.

Visit York's 'Full Visitor Guide' gives detailed, informative listings of hotels and other types of accommodation. You can download it from **www.visityork.org/**

The online service clearly shows vacancies and prices plus often considerable, helpful detail about the accommodation in question – like policy on pets.

- Note the search option for ranking accommodation by price.
- Note the search option for choosing distance from city centre.

One caution – people who don't know Yorkshire place names should check hotel addresses on the helpful map on this website, for this list can include occasional entries which are some distance from York.

Another caution concerns hotels on Micklegate. On Friday and Saturday nights, there are often many drunk or rowdy young people in the major York street, Micklegate, especially near its junction with George Hudson Street. This can create noise for hotel rooms facing on to Micklegate. Also, whilst in the author's experience these crowds are not at all dangerous, some people will prefer not to need to walk through this area at these times.

Between Visit York's on-line accommodation finder and TripAdvisor, you'll get information which is more up-to-date and customised to your preferences than any guidebook's list of recommendations. However, as follows, here are some places to stay which have special character.

Some noteworthy hotels and hostels
Here are five establishments which could be worth investigating via Visit York on-line / TripAdvisor because they are in either picturesque historic buildings or attractive locations or both. All but the last one listed are close to York's historic centre.

Higher price hotels

Middletons Hotel, Skeldergate, York YO1 6DS. Tel 01904 611570
www.middletonsyork.co.uk

The 56 bedroom Middletons Hotel is in a charming set of mainly Georgian and Victorian former commercial or residential buildings with a secluded, garden feel. Close to City Walls.
Map section: D5

Grange Hotel, 1 Clifton, York YO30 6AA. Tel 01904 644744
www.grangehotel.co.uk
The 36 bedroom Grange Hotel is in a sumptuous clergyman's mansion from the Georgian period, the era of York's fashionable Assembly Rooms social scene.
Map section: B1

Grays Court Hotel, Chapter House Street, York YO1 7JH. Tel 01904-612613.
www.grayscourtyork.com/
In a 17th century grand house with eight bedrooms, the family-run Grays Court hotel adjoins a lovely stretch of City Wall, near the Minster, and has a fine garden. A lengthy TV programme was created out of the roller-coaster drama of its recent launch as a hotel.
Map section: E2

Mid-price guesthouse
Bar Convent, 17 Blossom Street, York YO24 1AQ. Tel 01904-643238.
www.bar-convent.org.uk/accommodation.htm
The Bar Convent is an 18th century 'secret convent' whose museum (Chapter 2) shows how Catholics practiced their religion covertly during centuries of Protestant persecution. As a sideline, 18 rooms in this present day Catholic Convent provide Bed & Breakfast for tourists. Near Rail Station and Micklegate Bar on City Walls.
Map section: B6

Budget price hostel
York Youth Hostel, Water End, Clifton, York, North
Yorkshire, YO30 6LP. **Tel 0845 3719051**
www.yha.org.uk/hostel/york
York Youth Hostel offers both ensuite private rooms and
bunk-bed dormitories in a Victorian house with modern
interior and pleasant garden. A key thing is its unusual,
rural location near the path along the River Ouse, 25 / 30
minutes walk from York's City Walls, amid greenery in all
directions. Whether you walk to York along the river bank
footpath or via the attractive street, Bootham, in good
weather you'll enjoy it.
Map location: Off Central York map, north bank of Ouse
upstream from A2.

Restaurant clusters and cafés
Here are some places where there are so many restaurants
close together that you can be sure of finding a table.

In George Hudson Street (Map C4), off Micklegate and
near the Station, are some large foreign restaurants close
together: Indian, Chinese, Japanese, Thai and Turkish.

The long street which starts as Fossgate (Map E4) and
continues as Walmgate (F5) has more than 12 restaurants or
eateries of varied size, price and cuisine. More are opening
here each year and this street is fast becoming York's major
place for food. But, while it is near York's centre, its
entrance can be easily missed by visitors. Near the entrance
are Indian restaurants, a large new Spanish tapas bar and
the famous miniature pub, 'The Blue Bell'. Most of the
restaurants are a little further from York's centre, over the
little bridge into Walmgate, and include a large Scottish fish
restaurant, a rare Argentinian restaurant and Thai, Italian
and Polish establishments. Ever more bars and restaurants
are appearing in Fossgate / Walmgate since 2016 – it's hard
to keep track.

Nearer the station, the Micklegate Bar end of Micklegate (map B5) hosts another restaurant cluster in an attractive old street. At 112 Micklegate is 'Partisan', a coffee shop and restaurant fast gaining a cult following among Yorkies for imaginative multicultural food and quirky ambience.

Goodramgate (map E3) is another old street which is becoming a focus for bars and restaurants.

Chapter Two includes a section on restaurants and pubs in historic buildings.

For a review of York cafés, see this hard-to-beat web page, produced to support November's festival of short films: **www.asff.co.uk/while-in-york/**

Banks, post office etc

Overseas visitors, in Parliament Street (map E4) or in adjacent side streets you can find branches of all the main UK banks, while the main Post Office is just round the corner, off St Helen's Square (D3). Central York is very, very small. Everything you need is only a few steps walk away and you can find it simply by asking people.

Specialised guided tours of York

York Minster special tours Stained glass and stone repair workshop and hidden parts of Minster – see its website.

http://stainedglasscentre.org/ Tours of stained glass in York. Also, based in a disused medieval church in Micklegate, one-day practical courses in making stained glass.

www.yorkwalk.co.uk/ Guided walks round York on a wide variety of specialised history themes. Also sometimes coach tours further afield.

Mr. Punch has to listen for a change!
Punch & Judy puppet show in Parliament Street

Shock encounter with Mr Invisible!

Street entertainers

A wide variety of street entertainers come and go in York – singers, conjurors, acrobats etc. In Parliament Street (map E4), Kings Square (E3) and sometimes in St Helen's Square (D3), you may find performances before quite large audiences by street entertainers who mix conjuring tricks or acrobatics with a large dollop of clowning. At school half-term holidays such performances seem especially common. Singers and musicians can pop up anywhere – outside the Minster (D2/3) and in Low Petergate (D3) are common places. There are a couple of silent performers beside whom tourists like to have their photo taken. For instance there's a completely purple man who is sometimes parked motionless on a bicycle in Stonegate (D3). Nearby, round the corner in Petergate (D3), may lurk the faceless Mr Invisible.

York's 'Ghost Walks'

Many visitors seek out the evening Ghost Walks round parts of the York's Walled City. There are at least five competing Ghost Walks. They last 70 – 90 minutes and cost £4 or £5 for adults and £2 or £3 for children (2017 prices). Most Ghost Walks start at 7.30 pm. Each starts from its own separate place – like outside the Minster, in the Shambles etc. From the Visit York office you can get a leaflet about each walk and make your choice. Ghost Walks differ in the number of evenings per week that they are run and naturally this can vary across the seasons.

On TripAdvisor, you can see for yourself that the great majority of reviews about York's Ghost Walks are favourable – often strongly favourable. But a steady minority are critical.

Ghost Walks began as night time walking tours in historic cities, where a guide tells atmospheric stories of sensational

The Shambles: a narrow, dark, medieval street – the scene of many a Ghost Walk

historical or legendary events which have occurred at places along the route.

But some of York's Ghost Walks have branched out in different directions. To be frank, while the author's family had much enjoyed storytelling Ghost Walks in Edinburgh, the two York Ghost Walks, which we sampled, were very disappointing in comparison. The York guides failed to mention engrossing historical tales about places we walked past. Instead of good stories, they used slapstick clowning to engage their audience. That was many years ago but in recent TripAdvisor reviews our criticisms are repeated precisely. For certain stunts to be continued, in spite of repeated criticism on TripAdvisor, presumably some people must enjoy the very things which others dislike.

If considering a Ghost Walk:
- Compare recent TripAdvisor reviews before choosing your Ghost Walk. You best know your own tastes!

- If informed storytelling is what you are seeking, 'The Bloody Tour of York' is a Ghost Walk which pledges to provide this. Noticeably, it does not get criticism on TripAdvisor about the behaviour of the guide. Additionally, one of the guides on 'The Original Ghost Walk of York' gets repeated praise as a skilful storyteller.

- Before paying, consider the number of fellow walkers accumulating at the Ghost Walk assembly point. Sometimes the party becomes much too large for everyone to hear the guide or to fit into some of Old York's more interesting nooks and crannies.

Transport near York – and the excellent Yorkshire Travel.Net service

Most important - within York's compact Old Town, walking is much the easiest way to get around. Not only do you not need a car, but with pedestrianised streets and scarce parking a car can be a downright nuisance.

'Park and Ride' services

York is ringed with five such services. They enable you to park for free in secure car parks on York's outskirts, then travel into the city centre by frequent buses. For locations: **www.york.gov.uk/parking/ride/**

Park and pay

The Visit York map shows major car parks for the old town.

Taxi Ranks

Railway Station, St Saviourgate (near DIG), Duncombe Place (near Minster's west front), St Leonards Place (near Art Gallery), Tower Street (near Cliffords Tower). More detail: **www.york.gov.uk/transport/Taxis/Taxi_ranks/**

Public Transport – and YorkshireTravel.Net

Extremely helpful information is supplied by the website **www.yorkshiretravel.net/-** or phone 0871-200-22-33. You enter your destination and date and this website will supply detailed timetables of options for combinations of buses, trains, coaches and walking. While this guidebook includes only three destinations for which transport is necessary, YorkshireTravel.Net is valuable for the day trips to Dales and Coast which are mentioned at the end of this book.

Bus stops for excursions

- For Scarborough, Whitby, Bridlington and Castle Howard in one direction and Leeds in the other: there are bus stops outside the Rail Station and

Stonebow. On warm weekends, when many people are heading to the coast, queue outside the Rail Station lest the bus be full at Stonebow.

- For Beverley and Hull: the Rail Station and Merchantgate (near Merchant Adventurers Hall).

- For Ripon and Fountains Abbey: Picadilly (opposite Merchant Adventurers Hall).

- For Thirsk and Helmsley: St Leonards (near Art Gallery).

When to visit York: good times and bad times

York can be visited enjoyably all year round – though at its best in the warm May to August period. Most of its attractions are open almost all of the year and plenty are indoors. Attractive seasonal events occur as follows.

- February's Viking Festival and June's Roman Festival, both at schools half-term holidays, are very popular. See **Festival Calendar**.
- Mid-March to mid-April, York gets many visitors to see the many daffodils planted beside the City Walls.
- July's 'Great Yorkshire Fringe' is a new, lengthy festival of stand-up comedy, music, magic and some children's events. It is fast becoming the keystone of the York festival year. See **Festival Calendar**.
- Early December is a time when many British people make day trips to York, because the city radiates traditional English Christmas atmosphere. Some British people visit York to build up a Christmas mood in themselves.

Then there are three unusual events which could interest people with specialised interests: the Open Studios citizen artist weekends in April, York University's fortnight-long 'Festival of Ideas' in June, and the Aesthetica four-day festival of short films in early November. For descriptions and dates see this chapter's **Festival Calendar**.

Every four years, the spectacular medieval York Mystery Plays are performed on wagons open-air around central York. These plays are described in detail earlier this chapter, together with the date of the next performance and a contact website for details.

Less good times to visit

- If there is a bad period to visit York, it's between Christmas and mid-January since more things are closed than at any other time.

- If there is a bad day to visit York, it could be a Saturday during one of the four annual Ebor horseracing meetings at York's racecourse. Google 'Ebor races' for forthcoming dates. Hotels, taxis and restaurants can get full up and from late afternoon onwards the streets can get crowded with loud or drunken people. Though these racegoers come eye-catchingly dressed and some people view them as another of York's sights.

Also, in mid-2015 the *Guardian* newspaper publicised criticisms that on Saturdays, late afternoon and evening, central York was becoming unpleasant owing to organised parties of hard-drinking visitors from other towns. You may notice single gender parties of either young women or not so young men, often celebrating a Hen or Stag night. The epicentre for Saturday drunkenness is where George Hudson Street meets Micklegate and Bridge

Street (top side of map square C5 on standard tourist map of York). Generally these people do not pose any threat to other visitors to York. But some readers might wish to avoid these crowds.

However, as the next item clarifies, news about floods isn't a compelling reason to postpone a trip to York.

Flooding in York

Climate change has been bringing unprecedented flooding to Yorkshire. Autumn and winter is when this most often occurs. Concerning York, two crucial things to know:

1) Flooding from the large River Ouse usually has surprisingly little impact on a visit to York. Almost everything stays open, though the floods can be spectacular and you may see 'disaster sightseers' with cameras on Ouse bridges. But everything in this book usually stays accessible and open. Only one entry in this book is regularly affected – the 'Riverside and racecourse history walk' in Chapter 2. The author lives in York and can tell you authoritatively how limited is the impact of these floods.

2) The disastrous River Foss flood of late December 2015, which did close some major York tourist sights for a long while, was the result of man-made failure to service the River Foss flood barrier and not due to unpredictable natural forces. Thus repetition can easily be prevented, if the government restores funding as promised recently.

Curiously, even at the height of the December 2015 floods, it was still possible to visit most things in York – as long as you stayed on foot. Behind the Castle Museum, crowds gawked at the swelling waters where the River Foss flows into the River Ouse. Inside the Museum, as many people were touring it as usual. News of floods is certainly not a reason to cancel a planned visit to York.

Reducing admission costs: free entry attractions and the York Pass

Free attractions listed in this book
- National Rail Museum (Chapter 4).
- City Walls walk (Chapter 3), aside from entry to towers.
- The 'York's Old Streets' section of Chapter 2.
- The 'cat sculpture trail' (Chapter 2) seems currently to attract attention among families.
- Churches mentioned in Chapter 2 like All Saints North street, Holy Trinity Goodramgate and St Michael Le Belfry.
- The Guildhall (Chapter 2).
- York St Mary's Arts Centre (Chapter4)
- Museum Gardens (Chapter 4).
- The Riverside and Racecourse History Walk (Chapter 2).

Free entry for children (under 16 years)
York Minster (Chapter 1), Merchant Adventurers' Hall & Fairfax House (Chapter 2), Castle Museum, Yorkshire Museum & Art Gallery (Chapter 4).

Free entry for National Trust members
Treasurer's House and Goddards (see Riverside and Racecourse History Walk) – both in Chapter 2.

Free entry for English Heritage members
Nuclear War Observation bunker (Chapter 2), Cliffords Tower (Chapter 3).

The York Pass and other cheap combination tickets

Visit York sells the 'York Pass' which gives entry to 30 plus attractions inside and outside York. Adult / Child Passes cost, respectively, £40 / £26 for one day, £55 / £30 for two days and £65 / £35 for three.

The York Pass can also be bought on-line from **www.yorkpass.com**, which lists the many attractions which the Pass accesses plus side-benefits, some important small print, and periodic on-line discounts.

The York Pass certainly gets praised by some visitors. It does cover just about everything most worth seeing within York. But savings against ordinary admission prices are more easily made on the two-day Pass than the one-day version. And the case for the Pass is nothing like clear-cut.

Sometimes advertising has exaggerated savings through overstating how many visits can enjoyably be squeezed in timewise and through overlooking important cheap deals on ordinary admission tickets.

In calculating likely savings, bear in mind:

- Some York Pass attractions which are far from York, like Castle Howard, need at very least half a day including travel.

- For the Minster, Castle Museum, Yorkshire Museum and Fairfax House, children get free entry anyway.

- Very important, for the Minster, Fairfax House, Jorvik, DIG, Barley Hall and the Micklegate Bar Museum, via the ordinary admission tickets you can return *without further charge any time throughout the next 12 months*. Whereas entry via the York Pass is for the duration of that Pass only.

- Some ordinary tickets give Concession rates for people aged over 60, students, or people on Jobseeker's Allowance. But the York Pass does not. Some attractions also offer Family Tickets.

- Some of York's finest sights are free – like the City Walls, Rail Museum and old streets like Stonegate. When would you fit these in?

You also need to take account of other cheap combination tickets for clusters of York museums. There's one York Archaeological Trust cheap combination ticket which covers DIG, Jorvik, Barley Hall and the Richard III Museum and Micklegate Bar Museum and yet another for Jorvik and DIG only. Then there's York Museums Trust's cheap combination ticket for the Castle Museum, Yorkshire Museum and Art Gallery, which gives 12 month repeat entry. (See weblinks at their entries in this book.) If visiting York again the same year, such combination tickets could be money very well spent.

Much comes down to your own tastes when visiting historic attractions. If you're someone who likes to go slow and look at things carefully, you probably may not want to squeeze in enough attractions for the York Pass to make sense. But, if you like to move round fast and try to see or photograph as much as possible, the York Pass could be just the thing for you.

You need to work out what you want to see and have time to see, and calculate for yourself whether you would make savings through the Pass.

Ready-made day visit programme

If you don't want to spend time reading and choosing what to see in York, here is a ready-made programme which gives a good varied sample of York's heritage during a single day trip:

- **York Minster** in Chapter One.

- The **York's Old Streets** section of Chapter Two, maybe popping into the **Roman Bath**.

- The **Bootham Bar to Monk Bar** section of the City Walls in Chapter Three.

- *One* of the following museums from Chapter Four: **Railway Museum**, **Castle Museum** (North Building only) or **Jorvik** plus **DIG** since Jorvik is a fairly short visit and DIG is related subject matter and nearby.

- If you've any spare time, then **Museum Gardens** in Chapter Four.

If you pick the free entry Railway Museum, then your only admission charges would be for adults at the Minster (children enter free there) plus the low cost Roman Baths. If coming by train, note that the Railway Museum is near the station and generally stays open longer than anything else, so it might suit your last visit of the day.

The first three items listed are located close together.

Day trips from York to nearby places

An excellent source of comprehensive information is a huge e-book also by the author: *Choice Visits in Yorkshire and York*. It can be viewed and bought on: **www.amazon.co.uk/dp/B007P269ZQ**.

Every place it describes can be visited as a day trip from both York and Leeds – and almost always by public transport.

This e-book's Yorkshire day trips take you to stately homes and gardens, seaside and mountain walks, castles, caves, natural wonders, unusual museums, beaches and boat trips. Explore the book's large online free sample.

Within the latter book, the following are the quickest day trips from York – reachable within an hour's travel or less. Find bus and train times via **www.yorkshiretravel.net**

- **Beningbrough Hall** – fully described at the end of Chapter 2 in the book you are reading.

- **Burnby Hall Garden** at Pocklington is renowned for its water lily pool. It sells fish food for the pool's many friendly carp, who will actually eat it from your hand. Reachable by bus from York.

- **Scarborough** is a seaside town with attractions for every taste – a castle, seaside donkey rides, an aquarium and sea-life centre, boat trips to watch seals at sea, and astonishing miniature naval battles staged on a park pond. It takes a whole chapter of *Choice Visits in Yorkshire and York* to cover Scarborough's varied attractions. For a quick journey, go by train.

- **Knaresborough** is a lovely riverside town with a ruined castle, a historic witch's cave and a remarkable petrifying well which turns teapots and teddy bears to stone. From York, best reached by train.

- **Harrogate** is an elegant spa town with spa museum and spa gardens. From York, best reached by train.

- From Harrogate, it's a pleasant walk through the spa era Valley Gardens to **RHS Harlow Carr Gardens**.

- From Harrogate's bus station (very near the rail station), it's a quick bus ride onwards to **Ripley Castle** stately home and gardens – which includes 'Log Heights' adventure rope and tree climbing for adults and children.

- The **James Herriot Vet's Museum** at Thirsk can be reached within an hour's bus travel from York, though the journey back often takes much longer. See the real vet's surgery where many of the famous stories actually happened.

- Set in a Second World War Prisoner of War Camp, **Eden Camp** is an astonishing recreation of wonderfully varied aspects of life on the Home Front during the Second World War. It can be reached in an hour on the bus route between York and Whitby.

THE END

INDEX

About maps of York

Overleaf is a double-page spread of the standard City Centre map - by kind permission from Visit York. Every entry in this book quotes a grid reference on this map.

Note the dark mottled areas which represent York's two rivers, the wide Ouse and the smaller Foss, which can only be crossed at the bridges shown. Note too the dash-marked line of the City Walls, extending almost all round central York. You can walk along its battlements as a means for travelling round York - see Chapter 3.

If you want a map which is larger, more detailed and in colour, you can apply the same grid references in this book to any of the York maps available from Visit York. From **www.visityork.org/information/maps-of-york.aspx**   you can download the PDF of the 'York City Centre map' and print it out.

Alternatively you can obtain a paper map from Visit York's office or places like Park & Ride sites, hotels and museums. You can find a small version in the monthly free 'What's On? York Guide' available from Visit York. All these maps use the same grid references as this book.

For York outside the City Centre, download the 'York City Area' map from the same link cited above. For any of the day trips from York, mentioned in the final two pages of text, download the 'Surrounding Area' map.

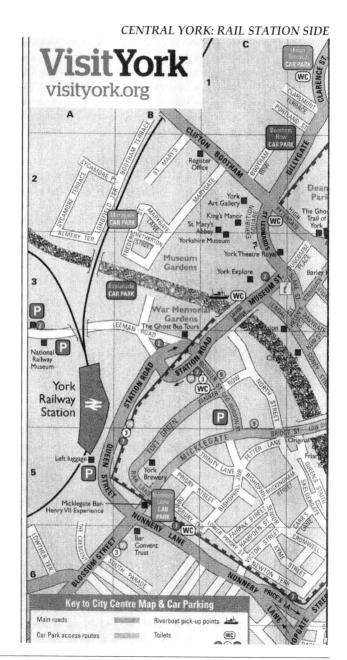

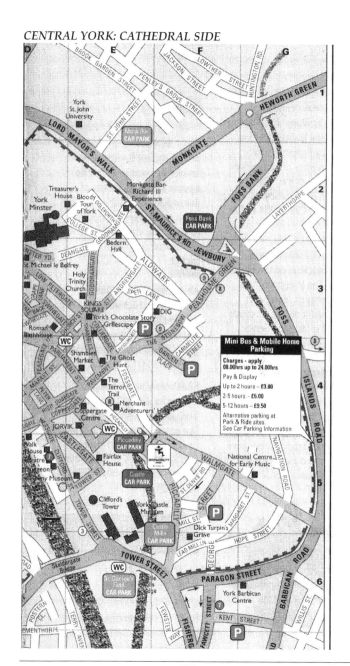

38158762R00102

Printed in Great Britain
by Amazon